Words of Remembrance and Words of Reminder

By
Dr. Saalih ibn Ghaanim al-Sadlaan
Professor, Muhammad ibn Saud Islamic University

Translated by
Jamaal al-Din M. Zarabozo

ذكر وتذكير

تأليف: الدكتور الأستاذ صالح بن غانم السدلان

نقله إلى الإنجليزية: جمال الدين زربوزو

1998

Words of Remembrance and Words of Reminder
By Saalih ibn Ghaanim al-Sadlaan

Published by:
Al-Basheer Company for Publications and Translations
1750 30th St. PMB #440
Boulder, CO   80301
U.S.A.

(Note: Not affiliated with Basheer Publications)

ISBN 1-891540-03-3 $9.00 Softcover (with audio tape)

Translator's Preface

Verily, all praise is due to Allah. We praise Him, seek His help and ask for His forgiveness. We seek refuge in Allah from the evil in our own souls and from our sinful deeds. Whoever Allah guides, no one can mislead. And whomever Allah allows to go astray, no one can guide. I bear witness that there is none worthy of worship except Allah, the One, having no partner. And I bear witness that Muhammad is His servant and messenger. O believers! Have fear of Allah according to His right and die not save as Muslims. O mankind! Have fear of your Lord, the One who created you from one soul and created from it its mate and from them spread many men and women. And fear Allah from whom you demand your mutual rights and [do not cut off] ties of kinship. Surely, Allah is Ever an All-Watcher over you. O Believers! Have fear of Allah and always speak the truth. He will direct you to righteous deeds and will forgive you your sins. And whosoever obeys Allah and His Messenger has indeed achieved a great achievement.

To proceed: Verily, the truest speech is the Book of Allah. The best guidance is the guidance of Muhammad. The worst affairs are the innovated ones. Every innovated matter is a heresy. And every heresy is misguidance. And every misguidance is in the Hell-fire.

In this small booklet, Dr. al-Sadlaan has combined together some of the most important words of *dhikr* (remembrance) that a person should adhere to in his daily life. However, in addition to that, he has made his work of even more importance by including in it words of reminder— that is, reminders of how one should behave and reminders of what one must refrain from in his daily life. We ask Allah to reward Dr. al-Sadlaan for his efforts and to make this book of benefit for Muslims as a whole.

It is preferred to say the words of *dhikr* in their original Arabic. There are many benefits to stating the words in Arabic. Among these benefits is that it brings the person closer to the language of the Quran itself as it slowly develops and builds his vocabulary. Furthermore, the person will be stating the exact words as taught by the Prophet (peace be upon him) and not a translation which may or may not capture the essence of the original Arabic.

For the above reasons, the original Arabic has been offered to the reader in three forms. First, the Arabic text of the words of *dhikr* is offered in the text with all of their vowel points. Second, for those who are not able to read Arabic, a strict transliteration of the Arabic wording is offered in the footnotes.[1] Third, a tape has been produced to accompany this work. The tape contains all of the authentic words of *dhikr* found in this book.[2]

The vowel sounds in Arabic are either short or long vowel sounds. The short vowel sounds are:

$$= a$$

$$= i$$

$$= u$$

These vowel sounds can also be made long as in the following:

---

[1] A strict method of transliteration with a unique mapping of each Arabic letter is only followed for the words of *dhikr*. For other Arabic words in the text, a looser method of transliteration has been followed.

[2] The tape has a number of advantages to it. First, transliteration usually proves very ineffective. This translator is a convert to Islam and such was his own personal experience. This is also what he has seen from others. Many times, it is very difficult to later correct one's mistaken attempt at trying to correctly pronounce transliterated text. Second, the tape can also be used by the reader separately to help him or her memorize the different words of *dhikr*.

ا ٔ   = *aa*

ي ِ   = *ee*

و ُ   = *oo*

These vowel sounds may be used in combination to form the following diphthongs:

و   = *au*

ي   = *ai*

The Arabic language has many consonant sounds that are pronounced in virtually the same manner as those found in English. Those sounds include the following[1]:

ب   = *b* as in boy or in the Arabic *bait*

ت   = *t* as in toy or in the Arabic *taaj*

ث   = *th* as in think or through (but not as in these) or in the Arabic *thaabit*

ج   = *j* as in joy or in the Arabic *jinn*

د   = *d* as in door or in the Arabic *daar*

ذ   = *dh* which is very close to the "th" sound in "the" or "then" or in the Arabic *dhaalika*

ز   = *z* as in zoo or in the Arabic *zauj*

س   = *s* as in sip (but not like a "z" sound as in

---

[1] The presentation below also shows the exact form of transliteration that is followed in the footnotes to the text. For some of the examples of equivalent English or European words, this translator benefited from J. Smart, *Teach Yourself Arabic: A Complete Course for Beginners* (Chicago: NTC Publishing Group, 1992), pp. 9-11.

                          "these") or in the Arabic *soorah*

ش   = _sh_ as in shoe or in the Arabic *shurooq*

ف   = *f* as in farm or in the Arabic *firaaq*

ك   = *k* as in kitchen or in the Arabic *kamaal*

ل   = *l* as in lamb or in the Arabic *labaika*

م   = *m* as in mind or in the Arabic *min*

ن   = *n* as in new or in the Arabic *noor*

ه   = *h* as in house or in the Arabic *huwa*

و   = *w* as in was or in the Arabic *witr*

ي   = *y* as in yes or in the Arabic *yaum*

The following sounds do not really have any equivalent in English. One should try to listen very closely to the tape to get their exact pronunciation:

ء   = ء[1] is a glottal stop and will be pronounced as a short vowel sound "a," "i" or "u" depending on the vowel over it; if there is no vowel over it, it acts like a brief stop in one's speech; some examples in Arabic include ʿ*akbar*, ʿ*inna* and *ba* ʿ*s*

ح   = *h* is a sound that is pronounced deep in the throat; an example in Arabic is *haamid*

خ   = _kh_ is similar to the ending of the German

---

1 For lack of a better or less confusing transliteration, the *hamza* has simply been left as it is in Arabic.

word *doch* or the Arabic _khurooj_

ر   = *r* is not exactly like the English "r" but is closer to the Spanish r in the word *pero*; an example in Arabic is *reem*

ص   = *s* as found in the Arabic *salaat*

ض   = *d* as found in the Arabic *daaleen*

ط   = *t* is a hard t sound as found in the Arabic word *taariq*

ظ   = *DH* as found in the Arabic word DH*aalim*

ع   = ' is like a tense glotal stop; an example is Arabic is *'arab*

غ   = *g* is somewhat similar to the French "r" sound; an example in Arabic is *gair*

ق   = *q* is somewhat similar to the way the letter "c" is pronounced in the word English word "calm"; an example in Arabic is *qur ʿan*

Those readers who are capable of reading but not quite understanding the Arabic text directly should also note that sometimes a hadith contains additional text other than the desired words of *dhikr*. In those cases, the actual words of *dhikr* in the Arabic text are marked by the following < >. If no such brackets are found in the Arabic text, it means that the entire Arabic text presented is the *dhikr* itself.

Before closing this introduction, I would like to express my gratitude to Dr. Sadlaan for his permission to translate this work. I would also like to extend my thanks to Br. Humaidan al-Turki who originally proposed the idea of translating this work. It is also Br. Humaidan, a specialist in Linguistics, whose voice is on the tape. I must also express my thanks to Br.

Nahar al-Rashid for his continued assistance. As always, I must thank my beloved wife for her patience and contribution to this work. I pray that Allah accepts all of their efforts and rewards them handsomely.

Jamaal al-Din M. Zarabozo
The translator
March 1, 1998

Table of Contents

AUTHOR'S INTRODUCTION...1

WORDS OF REMEMBRANCE AND WORDS OF REMINDER . 4

(1) THE VIRTUES AND BENEFITS OF THE REMEMBRANCE OF ALLAH. 4
Some of the Benefits of Dhikr...*5*
(2) THE WORDS OF REMEMBRANCE IN THE MORNING AND LATE
AFTERNOON 6
Specifying the Times of "Morn" and "Late Afternoon".................*6*
The Words of Remembrance for the Morning and Late Afternoon
are Many, Including:...*7*
(3) WHAT IS TO BE SAID AND DONE DURING THE NIGHTTIME.........15
(4) WORDS OF REMEMBRANCE THAT ARE NOT SPECIFIC FOR ANY
PARTICULAR TIME OR REASON 17
(5) RECITING THE QURAN...21
(6) WORDS OF REMEMBRANCE FOR THE TIME OF GOING TO SLEEP. 23
(7) WORDS OF REMEMBRANCE SAID WHEN ENTERING OR LEAVING
BATHROOMS 28
(8) WHAT IS SANCTIONED FOR BEFORE AND AFTER PERFORMING
ABLUTION 30
(9) WORDS OF REMEMBRANCE RELATED TO CLOTHING AND
DRESSING..31
(10) WORDS OF REMEMBRANCE RELATED TO ENTERING OR LEAVE
THE HOUSE..32
(11) WORDS OF REMEMBRANCE RELATED TO THE CALL TO PRAYER
....34
(12) WORDS OF REMEMBRANCE RELATED TO THE MOSQUE...........36
(12) WORDS OF REMEMBRANCE FOR AFTER THE RITUAL PRAYERS. 38
(14) WORDS OF REMEMBRANCE RELATED TO THE FAST..................42
(15) WORDS OF REMEMBRANCE FOR SPECIFIC OCCASIONS OR TIMES
THAT ARISE...44

(1) Salaat al-Istikhaarah (The Pray of Asking for Guidance on a Particular Matter)...........44
(2) The Prostration Upon Reciting the Quran 46
(3) The Prostration of Thankfulness...........46
(4) The Prayer of Repentance 47
(5) Upon Heading to the Mosque for the Morning (Fajr) Prayer 47
(6) During Hardship and Difficulties...........48
(7) When the Person Faces a Distressing Matter, Worry or Concern...........49
(8) If one Fears a People 50
(9) If a Matter Becomes Difficult or Hard for a Person...........50
(10) If Something Displeasing Happens to a Person...........51
(11) When a Person is Overcome by a Matter 51
(12) If One is Tried by Debt...........51
(13) If One is Afflicted with a Hardship...........52
(14) If a Person Has Some Doubt about Faith Occurring to His Mind...........52
(15) When One Feels the Disturbances of Satan while in Prayer, Reading the Quran and so forth...........53
(16) Words Said to Protect a Youngster...........53
(17) Upon Seeing Clouds about to Join Together...........53
(18) Upon Hearing the Sound of Thunder 54
(19) What to Say when the Winds Become Strong 54
(20) When it Rains...........54
(21) When it Rains a Great Deal or One Fears that it will Become Harmful...........55
(22) After Rainfall...........55
(23) Upon Seeing the New Moon 55
(24) When One Sees the Moonrise...........56
(25) When One Person Loves Another [For the Sake of Allah]...56
(26) When a Person Sees His Brother Laughing...........56
(27) Upon Sneezing...........57
(28) Upon Yawning...........58
(29) Upon Hearing a Donkey Braying or a Dog Barking...........58
(30) Upon Hearing a Rooster Crow...........58
(31) Before One Gets Up from a Gathering...........58
(32) Upon Getting Angry 59
(33) Upon Seeing One who is Being Afflicted...........59

(34) Upon Entering the Marketplace *60*
(35) When Someone Does a Good Deed For Another *60*
(36) Upon Repaying a Debt *61*
(37) Upon Seeing the First Fruits of Harvest *61*
(38) Upon Seeing Something Wonderful or Amazing *61*
(39) When One See Something that He Loves *62*
(40) When One Sees Something Disliked *63*
(41) Upon Purchasing a Riding Animal, Vehicle and So Forth .. *63*
(42) During Times of Difficulty, Grief or Worry *63*
(16) WORDS OF REMEMBRANCE RELATED TO THE ILL AND VISITING
THE SICK 66
(17) WORDS OF REMEMBRANCE RELATED TO TRAVEL 81
(18) WORDS OF REMEMBRANCE RELATED TO EATING AND DRINKING
.... 85
(19) WORDS OF REMEMBRANCE RELATED TO MARRIAGE AND
CONNECTED MATTERS 88
(20) GUARDING ONE'S TONGUE 89
(21) ABUSIVE LANGUAGE AND CURSING 100
(22) SOME REPREHENSIBLE TERMS 104
(23) STATEMENTS AND ACTIONS THAT ARE PROHIBITED FOR A
MUSLIM 105
(24) WILLS, BEQUESTS AND CHARITABLE ENDOWMENTS 113
(1) Wills and Bequests *113*
(2) Charitable Endowments *114*
(25) MENTION OF SOME ACTS OF EXPIATION 115
(1) The Expiation of One who Had Intercourse with His Wife
during the Daytime of Ramadhaan *115*
(2) The Expiation for al-Dhihaar *116*
(3) The Expiation for Breaking One's Oath *117*
(4) The Expiation for Breaking a Vow *118*
(5) The Expiation for One who Has Intercourse with His Wife
While She is Having Her Menses *119*
(6) What the Fasts of Arafah and Ashooraa Expiate *119*
(7) What the Prayers Expiate *120*
(7) What the Pilgrimage and Umrah Expiate *120*
(9) The Expiation for Useless Speech in a Gathering *121*
(26) THE VIRTUES OF SEEKING FORGIVENESS 121
(27) THE VIRTUES OF SUPPLICATIONS 123
The Etiquette of Supplications *124*

Those Whose Supplications are Answered.............................. *125*
Note... *126*

TRANSLATOR'S REFERENCES.. **127**

INDEX OF QURANIC VERSES CITED **129**

GENERAL INDEX.. **130**

Author's Introduction

All praise be to Allah who said in His Noble Book,

$$ وَذَكِّرْ فَإِنَّ ٱلذِّكْرَىٰ تَنفَعُ ٱلْمُؤْمِنِينَ $$

"And remind, for verily the reminder benefits the believers" (al-Dhaariyaat 55). He, Glorified be He, has said,

$$ إِنَّ فِى ذَٰلِكَ لَذِكْرَىٰ لِمَن كَانَ لَهُۥ قَلْبٌ أَوْ أَلْقَى ٱلسَّمْعَ وَهُوَ شَهِيدٌ $$

"Indeed, in that is a reminder for whoever has a heart or who listens while he is present [in mind]" (Qaaf 37). He, Glorified be He, has also said,

$$ فَذَكِّرْ بِٱلْقُرْءَانِ مَن يَخَافُ وَعِيدِ $$

"But remind by the Quran whoever fears My threat" (Qaaf 45). And I invoke blessings and peace upon the servant of Allah and His Messenger, the one who knew of no means to any good except that he indicated it to us and who knew of no path to evil except that he warned us of it.

To proceed:

My brother Muslim, in front of you is this small book entitled, Words of Remembrance and Words of Reminder. I have collected together in it the most important acts that a Muslim must or should do in a day and night. If a person acts by these deeds, as a believer and with sincere faith in them, he will have for him a fortress and citadel that will protect him from Satan and help him in repelling the evil of the jinn and the wrongdoers of mankind. When these words are stated with faith and conviction, they become a shield for him from every evil and disliked aspect. For that reason, one must become habitual and consistent in the saying of these words of remembrance. Furthermore, they must be said with a heart that is attentive and tranquil.

In addition, this small book also covers characteristics and praiseworthy attributes that every Muslim must have as part of his personality. The work also points out that which is foul speech and deeds that a Muslim must remain away from and avoid.

I have presented this book in a straightforward and easy to understand manner. I have [therefore intentionally] avoided some scholarly aspects, such as the following:

(1) I did not go into complete detail with respect to the matters concerning the recorders and grading of the hadith.[1]

(2) I restricted myself to simply mentioning the evidence from the hadith.

(3) I did not mention the name of the narrator of the hadith.

(4) I recorded some weak hadith which are not very weak or which have supporting evidence and which are related to the virtuousness of deeds.[2]

[These acts were done] for the sake of being brief. This is because this book is meant, first and foremost, for the general populous of Muslim men and women.

---

[1] Although such was the author's decision, this translator felt obliged to add at least some comment concerning the authenticity of the hadith quoted in this work, especially given the author's point number four above. However, in general, this comment is restricted to a reference to any one of the well-known scholars of hadith, past or present. It should also be noted that the transliterations in the footnotes and the recordings on the tape are only be given for those words that are based on acceptable hadith.—JZ

[2] On this point, the author is following the opinion of many well-known scholars. This translator holds a different view on this point and has discussed it in detail in his *Commentary on the Forty Hadith of al-Nawawi* (Boulder, CO: Basheer Company for Publications and Translations, forthcoming Allah willing). Therefore, the level of authenticity is noted in the relevant footnotes to each hadith in this book.—JZ

  Allah is the only One to ask to make this book beneficial for its author, reader and publisher.

  And may blessings of Allah and peace be upon our Prophet Muhammad, his family and his Companions.

Dr. Saalih ibn Ghaanim al-Sadlaan

Words of Remembrance and Words of Reminder

(1) The Virtues and Benefits of the Remembrance of Allah[1]

Allah says,

فَٱذۡكُرُونِيٓ أَذۡكُرۡكُمۡ وَٱشۡكُرُواْ لِى وَلَا تَكۡفُرُونِ

"So remember Me, I will remember you. And be grateful to Me and do not deny Me" (al-Baqara 152). He, exalted be He, has also said,

ٱلَّذِينَ ءَامَنُواْ وَتَطۡمَئِنُّ قُلُوبُهُم بِذِكۡرِ ٱللَّهِۚ أَلَا بِذِكۡرِ ٱللَّهِ تَطۡمَئِنُّ ٱلۡقُلُوبُ

"Those who have believed and whose hearts are made tranquil by the remembrance of Allah. Unquestionably, it is by the remembrance of Allah that the hearts can attain tranquillity" (al-Rad 28). He has also said,

فَلَوۡلَآ أَنَّهُۥ كَانَ مِنَ ٱلۡمُسَبِّحِينَ ۝ لَلَبِثَ فِى بَطۡنِهِۦٓ إِلَىٰ يَوۡمِ يُبۡعَثُونَ

---

[1] The Arabic word commonly used for the remembrance of Allah is *dhikr* (ذكر). That word shall be used throughout this book.—JZ

4

"And had he [Jonah] not been among those who exalt Allah, he would have remained inside its [the whale's] belly until the Day they are resurrected" (al-Saaffaat 143-144).

The Messenger of Allah (peace be upon him) said,

أَلاَ أُنَبِّئُكُمْ بِخَيْرِ أَعْمَالِكُمْ وَأَزْكَاهَا عِنْدَ مَلِيكِكُمْ وَأَرْفَعِهَا فِي دَرَجَاتِكُمْ

وَخَيْرٌ لَكُمْ مِنْ إِنْفَاقِ الذَّهَبِ وَالْوَرِقِ وَخَيْرٌ لَكُمْ مِنْ أَنْ تَلْقَوْا عَدُوَّكُمْ

فَتَضْرِبُوا أَعْنَاقَهُمْ وَيَضْرِبُوا أَعْنَاقَكُمْ قَالُوا بَلَى قَالَ ذِكْرُ اللَّهِ

"Shall I not inform you of the best of your deeds, the most sanctified in the sight of your Lord, that raises your ranks and that is better for you than spending in gold and money and better for you than meeting your enemy, striking their necks and them striking your necks?" They said, "Certainly [tell us]." He said, "It is the remembrance of Allah." (Recorded by al-Tirmidhi.[1])

Some of the Benefits of Dhikr[2]

(1) It repels, subdues and defeats Satan.
(2) It is pleasing to the Most Merciful, Allah.
(3) It removes worry and distress from the heart.
(4) It produces happiness, joy and pleasure for the heart.
(5) It erases and wipes away sins.
(6) It saves the human from being grieved on the Day of Resurrection.
(7) It is the seed for Paradise.

---

[1] According to al-Albani, this hadith is *sahih*. See Muhammad Naasir al-Deen al-Albani, *Sahih al-Jaami al-Sagheer* (Beirut: al-Maktab al-Islami, 1986), vol. 1, p. 512.—JZ

[2] On this topic, see the book *al-Waabil al-Sayyib* by Imam ibn al-Qayyim.

(2) The Words of Remembrance in the Morning and Late Afternoon

Specifying the Times of "Morn" and "Late Afternoon"

The times for the words of remembrance that are to be said in the morning and evening are at the beginning and at the end of the daytime; that is, they are the two ends of the daytime. The beginning of the day is from dawn until sunrise. The end of the day is from the time after *Asr* [mid-afternoon] until sunset. Allah says,

وَأَقِـــمِ ٱلصَّلَـــوٰةَ طَـــرَفَيِ ٱلنَّهَـــارِ وَزُلَفًـــا مِّـــنَ ٱلَّيۡـــلِّ إِنَّ ٱلۡحَسَــنَٰتِ يُـذۡهِبۡنَ ٱلسَّـيِّـَاتِۚ ذَٰلِـكَ ذِكۡرَىٰ لِلذَّٰكِـرِينَ

"And establish prayer at the two ends of the day and at the approach of the night. Indeed, good deeds wipe away evil deeds. That is a reminder for those who remember" (*Hood* 114). The Most High has also said,

وَسَبِّحۡ بِحَمۡدِ رَبِّكَ قَبۡلَ طُلُوعِ ٱلشَّمۡسِ وَقَبۡلَ

ٱلۡغُرُوبِ

"And exalt [Allah] with praises of your Lord before the rising of the sun and before its setting" (*Qaaf* 39).

Those two verses and others tells us what time is meant by the morn and late afternoon during the two times mentioned different hadith of the Prophet (peace be upon him). For example, the Prophet (peace be upon him) said,

مَنْ قَالَ حِينَ يُصْبِحُ وَحِينَ يُمْسِي < سُبْحَانَ اللَّهِ وَبِحَمْدِهِ > مِائَةَ

مَرَّةٍ لَمْ يَأْتِ أَحَدٌ يَوْمَ الْقِيَامَةِ بِأَفْضَلَ مِمَّا جَاءَ بِهِ إِلاَّ أَحَدٌ قَالَ مِثْلَ مَا

قَالَ أَوْ زَادَ عَلَيْهِ

"For whoever says, 'Exalted be Allah and to Him is the praise,[1]' one hundred times in the morning and in the late afternoon, no one will come on the Day of Resurrection with anything better than what he has done except for who said the same as he did or increased upon it." (Recorded by Muslim.)

If one is not able to mention those early morning or late afternoon words of *dhikr* in their aforestated times, there is no prohibition in him saying them after that time, if it be during the morning or evening.

The Words of Remembrance for the Morning and Late Afternoon are Many[2], Including:

(1) The Messenger of Allah (peace be upon him) said,

مَنْ قَالَ إِذَا أَصْبَحَ < لا إِلَهَ إِلاَّ اللَّهُ وَحْدَهُ لا شَرِيكَ لَهُ لَهُ الْمُلْكُ وَلَهُ

الْحَمْدُ وَهُوَ عَلَى كُلِّ شَيْءٍ قَدِيرٌ > كَانَ لَهُ عِدْلَ رَقَبَةٍ مِنْ وَلَدِ

إِسْمَاعِيلَ وَكُتِبَ لَهُ عَشْرُ حَسَنَاتٍ وَحُطَّ عَنْهُ عَشْرُ سَيِّئَاتٍ وَرُفِعَ لَهُ

---

[1] *Dhikr* #1: *Subhaanallaahi wa bihamdihi.*

[2] Al-Nawawi wrote, "If one is blessed and guided to perform all of these *dhikr*, it is great and a bounty from Allah and glad tidings for him. If a person cannot state all of them, then he should choose whichever of them he can perform, even if it is just one *dhikr*." See Yahya al-Nawawi, *al-Adhkaar* (Riyadh: Riaasah Idaarat al-Bahooth al-Ilmiyyah wa al-Iftaa wa al-Dawah wa al-Irshaad, 1981), p. 62.—JZ

عَشْرُ دَرَجَاتٍ وَكَانَ فِي حِرْزٍ مِنَ الشَّيْطَانِ حَتَّى يُمْسِيَ وَإِنْ قَالَهَا إِذَا

أَمْسَى كَانَ لَهُ مِثْلُ ذَلِكَ حَتَّى يُصْبِحَ

"Whoever says, 'There is none worthy of worship except
Allah, the One, for whom there is no partner. To Him belongs
the dominion and to Him is the praise. And He has power
over all things,'[1] in the early morning hours, for him will be
what is equivalent to freeing a slave from the descendants of
Ishmael; recorded for him will be ten good deeds; erased for
him will be ten evil deeds; he will be raised ten degrees; and
he will be protected from Satan until the late afternoon. If he
says it in the late afternoon, he will have a similar result until
the morning." (Recorded by Abu Dawood.[2])

(2) One should read the "Verse of the Throne" which
is,

ٱللَّهُ لَآ إِلَـٰهَ إِلَّا هُوَ ٱلْحَىُّ ٱلْقَيُّومُ لَا تَأْخُذُهُ سِنَةٌ وَلَا نَوْمٌ لَّهُ مَا فِى

ٱلسَّمَـٰوَٰتِ وَمَا فِى ٱلْأَرْضِ مَن ذَا ٱلَّذِى يَشْفَعُ عِندَهُ إِلَّا بِإِذْنِهِ يَعْلَمُ

مَا بَيْنَ أَيْدِيهِمْ وَمَا خَلْفَهُمْ وَلَا يُحِيطُونَ بِشَىْءٍ مِّنْ عِلْمِهِ إِلَّا بِمَا شَآءَ

وَسِعَ كُرْسِيُّهُ ٱلسَّمَـٰوَٰتِ وَٱلْأَرْضَ وَلَا يَـُٔودُهُ حِفْظُهُمَا وَهُوَ ٱلْعَلِىُّ

ٱلْعَظِيمُ

"Allah, there is none worthy of worship but Him, the Ever-
Living, the Sustaining. Neither drowsiness nor sleep overtakes
Him. To Him belongs whatever is in the heavens and the
earth. Who is it that can intercede with Him except by His
own permission? He knows what is before them and what is

---

[1] *Dhikr #2: La ṣilaaha ṣilla-llah, wahdahu laa shareeka lah, lahu-l-mulk wa
lahu-l-hamd, wa huwa 'ala kulli shai ṣin qadeer.*

[2] According to al-Albani, this hadith is *sahih*. See al-Albani, *Sahih al-Jaami*, vol. 2,
pp. 1095-1096.—JZ

behind them. They encompass nothing of His knowledge except for that which He wills. His Footstool extends over the heavens and the earth, and their preservation tires Him not. And He is the Most High, the Most Great" (*al-Baqara 255*). (Recorded by al-Nasaai and al-Tabaraani.[1])

---

[1] It seems, Allah knows best, that the author is referring to the hadith in al-Nasaai's *Sunan al-Kubra* in which Abu Huraira was put in charge of the dates given in charity. On three consecutive nights, someone came to steal some of that food. Abu Huraira caught him and told him that he would take him to the Prophet (peace be upon him). However, the man complained of his poverty. Mercy overtook Abu Huraira and he released him. The Prophet (peace be upon him) knew what had happened and told Abu Huraira that the person would come back. Finally, on the third night, the man told Abu Huraira that if he were to release him again he would teach him something beneficial. It was on that occasion that the person told Abu Huraira that if he were to recite the "Verse of the Throne" in the morning, it would protect him until the evening, and if he were to recite it in the late-afternoon, it would protect him until the morning. [See Ahmad ibn Shuaib al-Nasaai, *al-Sunan al-Kubra* (Beirut: Daar al-Kutub al-Imiyyah, 1991), vol. 5, pp. 13-14.] However, the more authentic narrations of that same incident, such as the narration in *Sahih al-Bukhari*, simply state the following, "If you let me go I will teach you some words by which Allah will greatly benefit you! When you go to your bed recite the verse of the throne [*al-Baqara* 255], from, 'Allah, there is no god but He, the Living, the Eternal,' to the end of the verse. If you do so a guardian from Allah will come and protect you from the devils until the morning." Al-Tabaraani has a similar story concerning Muadh ibn Jabal and, although there is mention of the "Verse of the Throne" in that hadith, there is no mention of reciting it in the morning and late-afternoon. [See Sulaimaan al-Tabaraani, *al-Mujam al-Kabeer* (Cairo: Maktaba ibn Taimiya, n.d.), vol. 20, pp. 51, 101 and 161-162.] Al-Tirmidhi has recorded a hadith which states, "Whoever recites *Ha Meem al-Mumin* until the words, 'And to Him is the journeying' [*Ghaafir* 1] and the 'Verse of the Throne' during the morning time will be protected due to them until the late afternoon. And whoever recites them in the late afternoon will be protected due to them until the morning." According to al-Albani, this hadith is weak. [See Muhammad Nasir al-Deen al-Albani, *Dhaeef Sunan al-Tirmidhi* (Beirut: al-Maktab al-Islami, 1991), pp. 341-342.] Al-Tabaraani also recorded something similar to that but his version only mentions reciting those verses and being protected for that day. Both of those narrations go through Abdul Rahman ibn Abu Bakr al-Mulaiki who was considered weak due to his poor memory. [See Sulaimaan al-Tabaraani, *Kitaab al-Duaa* (Beirut: Daar al-Bashaair al-Islaamiyah, 1987), vol. 2, p. 943.] Allah knows best.—JZ

(3) The Messenger of Allah (peace be upon him) said,

قُل قُلْ هُوَ اللَّهُ أَحَدٌ وَالْمُعَوِّذَتَيْنِ حِينَ تُمْسِي وَحِينَ تُصْبِحُ ثَلَاثًا يَكْفِيكَ مِنْ كُلِّ شَيْءٍ

"Say, 'Say: He is Allah alone,' [*Soorah al-Ikhlaas*] and the two *soorahs* of seeking refuge [the last two *soorahs* of the Quran] three times during the late afternoon and during the morning and it will suffice you from everything." (Recorded by Abu Dawood, al-Tirmidhi and al-Nasaai.[1])

(4) The Messenger of Allah (peace be upon him) also said,

سَيِّدُ الِاسْتِغْفَارِ أَنْ تَقُولَ < اللَّهُمَّ أَنْتَ رَبِّي لَا إِلَهَ إِلَّا أَنْتَ خَلَقْتَنِي وَأَنَا عَبْدُكَ وَأَنَا عَلَى عَهْدِكَ وَوَعْدِكَ مَا اسْتَطَعْتُ أَعُوذُ بِكَ مِنْ شَرِّ مَا صَنَعْتُ أَبُوءُ لَكَ بِنِعْمَتِكَ عَلَيَّ وَأَبُوءُ لَكَ بِذَنْبِي فَاغْفِرْ لِي فَإِنَّهُ لَا يَغْفِرُ الذُّنُوبَ إِلَّا أَنْتَ < قَالَ وَمَنْ قَالَهَا مِنَ النَّهَارِ مُوقِنًا بِهَا فَمَاتَ مِنْ يَوْمِهِ قَبْلَ أَنْ يُمْسِيَ فَهُوَ مِنْ أَهْلِ الْجَنَّةِ وَمَنْ قَالَهَا مِنَ اللَّيْلِ وَهُوَ مُوقِنٌ بِهَا فَمَاتَ قَبْلَ أَنْ يُصْبِحَ فَهُوَ مِنْ أَهْلِ الْجَنَّةِ

"The leader of the words of seeking forgiveness is for you to say: 'O Allah, you are my Lord, there is none worthy of worship except You. You created me and I am Your servant. I am according to Your covenant and Your Promise to the best of my ability. I seek refuge in You from the evil of what I have done. I recognize Your bounties that You have bestowed on me. I admit my sins, so forgive me, as no one forgives sins except You.' Whoever says that during the daytime, with firm belief in it, and dies on that day before the evening, he will be from the inhabitants of Paradise. And whoever says that during the night while believing firmly in it, and dies before

---

[1] According to Saleem al-Hilaali, this hadith is *hasan*. See Saleem al-Hilaali, *Sahih Kitaab al-Adhkaar wa Dhaeefuhu* (Madinah: Maktabah al-Ghurabaa al-Athariyyah, 1997), vol. 1, p. 220.—JZ

the morning, will be from the inhabitants of Paradise."
(Recorded by al-Bukhari.[1])

(5) The Prophet (peace be upon him) also said,

مَنْ قَالَ < بِسْمِ اللَّهِ الَّذِي لا يَضُرُّ مَعَ اسْمِهِ شَيْءٌ فِي الأَرْضِ وَلا فِي

السَّمَاءِ وَهُوَ السَّمِيعُ الْعَلِيمُ > ثَلاثَ مَرَّاتٍ لَمْ تُصِبْهُ فَجْأَةُ بَلاءٍ حَتَّى

يُصْبِحَ وَمَنْ قَالَهَا حِينَ يُصْبِحُ ثَلاثُ مَرَّاتٍ لَمْ تُصِبْهُ فَجْأَةُ بَلاءٍ حَتَّى

يُمْسِيَ

"Whoever says three times, 'In the name of Allah the One by
whose name nothing is harmed on the earth or in heaven.
And He is the All-Hearer, the All-Knower,'[2] no unexpected
trial will come to him until the early morning. And whoever
says it three times in the early morning will have no
unexpected trial come to him until the late afternoon."
(Recorded by Abu Dawood.[3])

(6) The Prophet (peace be upon him) also said,

مَنْ قَالَ حِينَ يُصْبِحُ وَحِينَ يُمْسِي ثَلاثَ مَرَّاتٍ < رَضِيتُ بِاللَّهِ رَبًّا

وَبِالإِسْلامِ دِينًا وَبِمُحَمَّدٍ صَلَّى اللَّهم عَلَيْهِ وَسَلَّمَ نَبِيًّا > إِلاَّ كَانَ حَقًّا

عَلَى اللَّهِ أَنْ يُرْضِيَهُ يَوْمَ الْقِيَامَةِ

"Whoever says three times when it becomes early morning
and when it becomes late afternoon, 'I am pleased with Allah
as Lord, with Islam as religion and with Muhammad, peace

---

[1] *Dhikr* #3: *Allahumma ʂanta rabbi laa ʂilaaha ʂillaa ʂanta. Khalaqtani wa
ʂana 'abduka wa ʂana 'ala 'ahdika wa wa'dika maa-stata'tu ʂa'oodhu bika
min sharri maa sana'tu. ʂaboo ʂu laka bini'matika 'alayya wa ʂaboo ʂu bi-
dhanbee fagfirlee fa ʂinnahu laa yagfiru-dhunooba ʂilla ʂanta.*

[2] *Dhikr* #4: *Bismillahi-lladhee laa yaḍurru ma'-smihi shai ʂun fi-l-ʂard wa laa
fee-samaa ʂ wa huwa as-samee'u-l-'aleem*

[3] According to al-Albani, it is *sahih.* See Muhammad Naasir al-Deen al-Albani,
Sahih Sunan Abi Dawood (Riyadh: Maktab al-Tarbiyyah al-Arabi li-Duwal al-
Khaleej, 1989), vol. 3, p. 958.—JZ

and blessings of Allah be upon him, as prophet,'[1] shall have a right upon Allah that he shall be made pleased on the Day of Resurrection." (Recorded by Ahmad and ibn al-Sunee.[2])

(7) The Prophet (peace be upon him) also said,

من صلى علي حين يصبح عشراً وحين يمسي عشراً أدركته شفاعتي

يوم القيامة

"Whoever prays for me ten times during the early morning and during the late afternoon will find my intercession on the Day of Resurrection." (Recorded by al-Tabaraani.[3])

(8) In the late afternoon, the Prophet (peace be upon him) would say,

< أَمْسَيْنَا وَأَمْسَى الْمُلْكُ لِلَّهِ وَالْحَمْدُ لِلَّهِ لا إِلَهَ إِلاَّ اللَّهُ وَحْدَهُ لا

شَرِيكَ لَهُ لَهُ الْمُلْكُ وَلَهُ الْحَمْدُ وَهُوَ عَلَى كُلِّ شَيْءٍ قَدِيرٌ رَبِّ أَسْأَلُكَ

خَيْرَ مَا فِي هَذِهِ اللَّيْلَةِ وَخَيْرَ مَا بَعْدَهَا وَأَعُوذُ بِكَ مِنْ شَرِّ مَا فِي هَذِهِ

اللَّيْلَةِ وَشَرِّ مَا بَعْدَهَا رَبِّ أَعُوذُ بِكَ مِنَ الْكَسَلِ وَسُوءِ الْكِبَرِ رَبِّ أَعُوذُ

بِكَ مِنْ عَذَابٍ فِي النَّارِ وَعَذَابٍ فِي الْقَبْرِ > وَإِذَا أَصْبَحَ قَالَ ذَلِكَ

أَيْضًا أَصْبَحْنَا وَأَصْبَحَ الْمُلْكُ لِلَّهِ

---

[1] *Dhikr #5: Radeetu bi-llaahi rabban wa bi-l-ṣislaami deenan wa bi-muhammadin salla-llaahu 'alaihi wa sallam nabiyyan.*

[2] Although the chain to this hadith has some weakness to it, al-Hilaali concludes that the hadith is *hasan* based on its supporting evidence. See al-Hilaali, vol. 1, p. 227.—JZ

[3] Al-Albani concludes that this hadith is *hasan*. (See al-Albani, *Sahih al-Jaami*, vol. 2, p. 1088.) On the other hand, Mashhoor Hasan Salmaan points out that there is some weakness in its chain, including the fact that the chain is broken. Salmaan, though, does not make any conclusion concerning the authenticity of the hadith. See Mashhoor Hasan Salmaan's footnotes to Abu Bakr ibn al-Qayyim, *Jalaa al-Afhaam fi Fadhl al-Salaat wa al-Salaam ala Muhammad Khair al-Anaam* (Dammam, Saudi Arabia: Dar ibn al-Jauzi, 1997), pp. 212-213.—JZ

"We have reached the evening and at this same time the dominion belongs to Allah and all praise is to Allah. There is none worthy of worship except Allah, the One alone who has no partner with Him. For Him is the dominion and to Him is the praise. And He has power over all things. Lord, I ask you for the good of this night and the good of what follows it. And I seek refuge in You from the evil of what is in this night and the evil of what follows it. Lord, I seek refuge in You from laziness and senility. Lord, I seek refuge in You from punishment in the Fire and punishment in the grave."[1] When he reached the morning, he would also say, "I have reached the early morning and..." (Recorded by Muslim.)

(9) The Prophet (peace be upon him) also said,

قُلِ < اللَّهُمَّ فَاطِرَ السَّمَوَاتِ وَالأَرْضِ عَالِمَ الْغَيْبِ وَالشَّهَادَةَ رَبَّ كُلِّ

شَيْءٍ وَمَلِيكَهُ أَشْهَدُ أَنْ لا إِلَهَ إِلاَّ أَنْتَ أَعُوذُ بِكَ مِنْ شَرِّ نَفْسِي وَشَرِّ

الشَّيْطَانِ وَشِرْكِهِ وَأَنْ أَقْتَرِفَ عَلَى نَفْسِي سُوْءً أَوْ أَجُرَّهُ إِلَى مُسْلِمٍ >

قَالَ قُلْهَا إِذَا أَصْبَحْتَ وَإِذَا أَمْسَيْتَ وَإِذَا أَخَذْتَ مَضْجَعَكَ

"Say: O Allah, creator of the heavens and the earth, knower of the unseen and seen, Lord of everything and its Sovereign, I bear witness that there is none worthy of worship except You. I seek refuge in You from the evil in my soul and from the evil of Satan and his ascribing of partners to Allah. [I also seek refuge from] acquiring any evil for myself or bringing such upon any Muslim."[2] Then the Prophet (peace be upon

---

[1] *Dhikr* #6: *ᶜamsainaa wa ᶜamsa al-mulku lilaahi wa al-hamdulilaah, laa ᶜilaaha ᶜilla-llah wahdahu laa shareeka lahu, lahu-l-mulku wa lahu-l-hamd, wa huwa 'ala kulli shai ᶜin qadeer, rabbi ᶜas ᶜaluka khaira maa fee haadhihi-llailah wa khaira maa ba'daha, wa ᶜaoodhu bika min sharr maa fee hadhihi-llailah wa sharr ma ba'daha, rabbi ᶜaoodhu bika min al-kasali wa soo ᶜi-l-kibar, rabbi ᶜaoodhu bika min 'adhaabun fee-n-naar wa 'adhaabun fee-l-qabr.* In the early morning *dhikr*, he would say the same words except the beginning would be: *ᶜasbahnaa wa ᶜasbaha al-mulku lilaah...*

[2] *Dhikr* #7: *Allahumma faatira-samaawaati wa-l-ᶜard, 'aalima-l-gaibi wa-shahaadah, rabba kulli shai ᶜin wa maleekahu, ᶜashhadu an laa ᶜilaaha ᶜilla*

him) said, "Say that when you are in the early morning, late afternoon and when you take to your bed." (Recorded by Ahmad and Abu Dawood.[1])

(10) The Prophet (peace be upon him) also said,

مَنْ قَالَ حِينَ يُصْبِحُ < اللَّهُمَّ مَا أَصْبَحَ بِي مِنْ نِعْمَةٍ فَمِنْكَ وَحْدَكَ لَا

شَرِيكَ لَكَ فَلَكَ الْحَمْدُ وَلَكَ الشُّكْرُ > فَقَدْ أَدَّى شُكْرَ يَوْمِهِ وَمَنْ قَالَ

مِثْلَ ذَلِكَ حِينَ يُمْسِي فَقَدْ أَدَّى شُكْرَ لَيْلَتِهِ

"Whoever says when the early morning comes, 'O Allah, whatever blessings I have in this morning are from You alone, You have no partner, so for You is the praise and for you are the thanks,' has fulfilled the obligation of thanks for that day. And whoever says the same when evening comes has fulfilled the obligation of thanks for his night." (Recorded by Abu Dawood.[2])

(11) One should say, "Exalted and glorified be Allah and for Him is the praise,"[3] one hundred times. (Recorded by Muslim.)

(12) When the late afternoon comes, one should say three times,

أَعُوذُ بِكَلِمَاتِ اللَّهِ التَّامَّاتِ مِنْ شَرِّ مَا خَلَقَ

"I seek refuge in Allah's complete and perfect words from the evil He has created."[4] (Recorded by Ahmad and al-Tirmidhi.[1])

---

anta, aoodhu bika min sharri nafsee wa sharri-shaitaani wa shirkihi, wa an aqtarifa 'ala nafsee soo an au ajurrahu ila muslim.

[1] According to al-Hilaali, this hadith is *sahih*. See al-Hilaali, vol. 1, pp. 223-224.—JZ

[2] According to both al-Albani and al-Hilaali, this hadith is weak. See Muhammad Naasir al-Deen al-Albani, *Dhaeef al-Jaami al-Sageer* (Beirut: al-Maktab al-Islaami, 1988), p. 825; al-Hilaali, vol. 1, p. 230.—JZ

[3] *Dhikr #8:* سُبْحَانَ الله وبِحَمْدِهِ *Subhaanallaahi wa bihamdihi.*

[4] *Dhikr #9: a'oodhu bi-kalimaati-laahi al-taamaat min sharri maa khalaq.*

(3) What is to be Said and Done During the Nighttime

(1) The person should read the last two verses of *soorah al-Baqara*, which are:

ءَامَنَ ٱلرَّسُولُ بِمَآ أُنزِلَ إِلَيْهِ مِن رَّبِّهِۦ وَٱلْمُؤْمِنُونَ ۚ كُلٌّ ءَامَنَ بِٱللَّهِ وَمَلَـٰٓئِكَتِهِۦ وَكُتُبِهِۦ وَرُسُلِهِۦ لَا نُفَرِّقُ بَيْنَ أَحَدٍ مِّن رُّسُلِهِۦ ۚ وَقَالُوا۟ سَمِعْنَا وَأَطَعْنَا ۖ غُفْرَانَكَ رَبَّنَا وَإِلَيْكَ ٱلْمَصِيرُ

لَا يُكَلِّفُ ٱللَّهُ نَفْسًا إِلَّا وُسْعَهَا ۚ لَهَا مَا كَسَبَتْ وَعَلَيْهَا مَا ٱكْتَسَبَتْ ۗ رَبَّنَا لَا تُؤَاخِذْنَآ إِن نَّسِينَآ أَوْ أَخْطَأْنَا ۚ رَبَّنَا وَلَا تَحْمِلْ عَلَيْنَآ إِصْرًا كَمَا حَمَلْتَهُۥ عَلَى ٱلَّذِينَ مِن قَبْلِنَا ۚ رَبَّنَا وَلَا تُحَمِّلْنَا مَا لَا طَاقَةَ لَنَا بِهِۦ ۖ وَٱعْفُ عَنَّا وَٱغْفِرْ لَنَا وَٱرْحَمْنَآ ۚ أَنتَ مَوْلَىٰنَا فَٱنصُرْنَا عَلَى ٱلْقَوْمِ ٱلْكَـٰفِرِينَ

"The Messenger has believed in what was revealed to him from his Lord, and [so have] the believers. All of them have believed in Allah and His angels and His books and His messengers, [saying,] 'We make no distinction between any of His messengers.' And they say, 'We hear and we obey. [We seek] Your forgiveness, our Lord, and to You is the destination.' Allah does not burden any soul beyond what it can bear. It will have for it what it has gained and against it what it has earned. 'Our Lord, do not impose blame upon us if we have forgotten or erred. Our Lord, lay not upon us a

---

1 This supplication will protect one from the harm of a snake bite during the following night. According to al-Albani, this hadith is *sahih*. See al-Albani, *Sahih al-Jaami*, vol. 2, p. 1097.

burden like that which You placed upon those before us. Our Lord, burden us not with that which we have no ability to bear. Pardon us, forgive us and have mercy upon us. You are our protector, so give us victory over the disbelieving people'" (*al-Baqara* 285-286). "Whoever recites that during the night, it will be sufficient for him."[1] (Recorded by al-Bukhari.)

(2) It is recommended that when the night begins for the person to do as the Prophet (peace be upon him) has said:

إِذَا جُنْحُ اللَّيْلِ فَكُفُّوا صِبْيَانَكُمْ فَإِنَّ الشَّيَاطِينَ تَنْتَشِرُ حِينَئِذٍ فَإِذَا ذَهَبَ سَاعَةٌ مِنَ الْعِشَاءِ فَخَلُّوهُمْ

"When the night just begins after sunset, bring your children in for the devils spread out at that time. After some time has passed, you may allow them to go out again..." (Recorded by al-Bukhari.)

(3) It is also recommended to recite *soorah al-Mulk* every night, based on the hadith,

من قرأ تبارك الذي بيده الملك كل ليلة منعه الله عز وجل بها من عذاب القبر

"Whoever recites, 'Blessed be the One in whose Hand is the Dominion' (*soorah al-Mulk*), every night will be prevented by Allah due to it from being punished in the grave." (Recorded by al-Haakim.[2])

(4) It is also recommended that when one wakes in the latter part of the night, before one performs the late-night prayers, to look towards the heavens and recite verses 190 to 200 of *soorah ali-Imraan*, "Verily, in the creation of the heavens and the earth..."

---

[1] This either means that it will protect him from any harm during that night or, it is said, it means that it suffices him from performing the late-night prayer that night.

[2] This hadith is *hasan* according to the conclusion of many scholars. See Fauzi ibn Abdullah ibn Muhammad, *Al-Fulk fi Fadhl Soorah al-Mulk*, pp. 11-17.

(4) Words of Remembrance that are Not Specific for any Particular Time or Reason

(1) A man said, "O Messenger of Allah, the laws of Islam are too many for me, so inform me of something that I may thereby cling to tenaciously." The Prophet (peace be upon him) told him,

لا يَزَالُ لِسَانُكَ رَطْبًا مِنْ ذِكْرِ اللَّهِ

"Let your tongue always be constantly wet by[1] the remembrance of Allah." (Recorded by al-Tirmidhi and Imam Ahmad. Ibn Hibbaan has declared it *sahih*, as did al-Haakim and al-Dhahabi agreed with him.[2])

(2) The Prophet (peace be upon him) also said,

مَنْ قَالَ > لا إِلَهَ إِلاَّ اللَّهُ وَحْدَهُ لا شَرِيكَ لَهُ لَهُ الْمُلْكُ وَلَهُ الْحَمْدُ وَهُوَ عَلَى كُلِّ شَيْءٍ قَدِيرٌ < فِي يَوْمٍ مِائَةَ مَرَّةٍ كَانَتْ لَهُ عَدْلَ عَشْرِ رِقَابٍ وَكُتِبَ لَهُ مِائَةُ حَسَنَةٍ وَمُحِيَتْ عَنْهُ مِائَةُ سَيِّئَةٍ وَكَانَتْ لَهُ حِرْزًا مِنَ الشَّيْطَانِ يَوْمَهُ ذَلِكَ حَتَّى يُمْسِيَ وَلَمْ يَأْتِ أَحَدٌ بِأَفْضَلَ مِمَّا جَاءَ إِلَّا رَجُلٌ عَمِلَ أَكْثَرَ مِنْهُ

"Whoever says, 'There is none worthy of worship except Allah, the One who has no partner with Him. To Him belongs the dominion and to Him is the praise. And He has power over all things,'[3] one hundred times in a day will have for him reward equivalent to freeing ten slaves, written for him will be one hundred good deeds, one hundred bad deeds will be erased for him and he will have a protection from Satan for his day until the evening. No one will do better than what

---

[1] Meaning, "Busy with, perpetual with."—JZ

[2] Also according to al-Albani, this hadith is *sahih*. See al-Albani, *Sahih al-Jaami*, vol. 2, p. 1273.—JZ

[3] *Dhikr* #10: *laa ꜱilaaha ꜱilla-llah, wahdahu laa shareek lahu, wa huwa 'ala kulli shai ꜱin qadeer.*

he has done except for one who does it more than him."
(Recorded by al-Bukhari.)

(3) One time the Messenger of Allah (peace be upon him) left the Mother of the Believers Juwairiyyah to go to the Morning Prayer and she was at her place of worship [inside the house]. He then returned after the sun had risen and she was still sitting in the same place. He said, "You are still in the position in which I had left you?" She said, "Yes." The Prophet (peace be upon him) then said,

$$ لَقَدْ قُلْتُ بَعْدَكِ أَرْبَعَ كَلِمَاتٍ ثَلَاثَ مَرَّاتٍ لَوْ وُزِنَتْ بِمَا قُلْتِ مُنْذُ الْيَوْمِ $$
$$ لَوَزَنَتْهُنَّ > سُبْحَانَ اللَّهِ وَبِحَمْدِهِ عَدَدَ خَلْقِهِ وَرِضَا نَفْسِهِ وَزِنَةَ عَرْشِهِ $$
$$ وَمِدَادَ كَلِمَاتِهِ < $$

"After you, I said four sentences three times. If what I did on this day is weighed against what you have done, it would outweigh it. [These sentences were,] 'Exalted and glorified be Allah and to Him is the praise to the number of His creation and what pleases Him, and the amount of the weight of His Throne and the number of His words.'[1]" (Recorded by Muslim.)

(4) The Prophet (peace be upon him) said,

$$ لَأَنْ أَقُولَ > سُبْحَانَ اللَّهِ وَالْحَمْدُ لِلَّهِ وَلَا إِلَهَ إِلَّا اللَّهُ وَاللَّهُ أَكْبَرُ < $$
$$ أَحَبُّ إِلَيَّ مِمَّا طَلَعَتْ عَلَيْهِ الشَّمْسُ $$

"For me to say, 'How exalted and perfect Allah is, all praise is due to Allah, there is none worthy of worship except Allah and Allah is the greatest,'[2] is more beloved to me than everything that the sun rises over." (Recorded by Muslim.)

(5) Abu Musa al-Ashari narrated that the Prophet (peace be upon him) said to him, "Shall I not inform you of a statement that is a treasure from the treasures of Paradise?"

---

[1] *Dhikr* #11: *Subhaanallaahi wa bihamdihi 'adada khalqihi wa ridaa nafsihi wazinata 'arshihi wa midaada kalimaatihi.*

[2] *Dhikr* #12: *Subhaanallaahi wa-l-hamdulilaah wa laa ɛilaaha ɛilla-llahu wallahu ɛakbar.*

Abu Musa answered, "Certainly." The Prophet (peace be upon him) then said,

لا حَوْلَ وَلا قُوَّةَ إلاَّ بِاللهِ

"There is no movement and no power except in Allah."[1] (Recorded by Muslim.)

(6) The Prophet (peace be upon him) once said, "Is any of you not able to earn in a day one thousand good deeds." One of the people sitting there said, "How can one of us earn one thousand good deeds?" The Prophet (peace be upon him) said,

يُسَبِّحُ مِائَةَ تَسْبِيحَةٍ فَيُكْتَبُ لَهُ أَلْفُ حَسَنَةٍ أَوْ يُحَطُّ عَنْهُ أَلْفُ خَطِيئَةٍ

"He exalts and hallows Allah one hundred times and has written for him one thousand good deeds or has removed one thousand sins from him." (Recorded by Muslim.)

(7) The Prophet (peace be upon him) also said,

وَاللهِ إِنِّي لأَسْتَغْفِرُ اللَّهَ وَأَتُوبُ إِلَيْهِ فِي الْيَوْمِ أَكْثَرَ مِنْ سَبْعِينَ مَرَّةً

"By Allah, I seek Allah's forgiveness and repent to Him more than seventy times in a day." (Recorded by al-Bukhari.)

(8) One must pray for the Prophet (peace be upon him) often as Allah has said,

إِنَّ اللَّهَ وَمَلَٰئِكَتَهُۥ يُصَلُّونَ عَلَى ٱلنَّبِيِّ يَٰٓأَيُّهَا ٱلَّذِينَ ءَامَنُوا۟ صَلُّوا۟ عَلَيْهِ وَسَلِّمُوا۟ تَسْلِيمًا

"Indeed, Allah confers blessings upon the Prophet, and His angels [also beseech Him to do so]. O believers, ask [Allah to confer] blessings upon him and grant him peace" (al-Ahzaab 56). The Prophet (peace be upon him) himself also said,

أَوْلَى النَّاسِ بِي يَوْمَ الْقِيَامَةِ أَكْثَرُهُمْ عَلَيَّ صَلاةً

---

[1] Dhikr #13: Laa haula wa laa quwwata ẹilla bi-llaah.

19

"The closest people to me on the Day of Resurrection are those who pray most for me." (Recorded by al-Tirmidhi.[1])
   The time and places in which one should state prayers for the Prophet (peace be upon him) include:[2]
   (1) Before and after supplicating to Allah.[3] (Recorded by Ahmad and Abu Dawood.)

---

[1] This hadith was recorded by a number of scholars but all with weak chains. The hadith revolve around Musa ibn Yaqoob. According to al-Daraqutni he is an unacceptable narrator and he is the source of the confused narrations of this hadith; he is a weak narrator who may be resorted to only for supporting evidence. Most of the chains also have some other slight problem with them. Hence, al-Albani, al-Hilaali, Salmaan and Shuaib al-Arnaoot state that this is a weak hadith. However, Salmaan and al-Arnaoot, following the lead of ibn Hajr, point out that there is another hadith narrated on the authority of Abu Umamah: "The prayers of my Nation for me are presented to me on every Friday. Those who pray the most for me have the closest position to me." It is probable that it also has a broken chain. The two narrations taken together could possibly support one another to raise the hadith to the level of *hasan* except that Musa ibn Yaqoob may be too weak of a narrator for that. Allah knows best. After recording this hadith, ibn Hibbaan stated, "In this report there is evidence that those people who will be closest to the Prophet (peace be upon him) on the Day of Resurrection are the scholars of hadith as no people from this nation state more prayers on the Prophet (peace be upon him) than them." See Ali ibn Umar al-Daaraqutni, *al-Ilal al-Waaridah fi al-Ahaadeeth al-Nabawiyyah* (Riyadh: Dar Taibah, n.d.), vol. 5, pp. 111-113; Ali al-Faarisi, *al-Ihsaan fi Taqreeb Saheeh ibn Hibbaan* (Beirut: Muasassah al-Risaalah, 1987), vol. 3, pp. 192-193; al-Albani, *Dhaeef al-Jaami al-Sagheer*, p. 262; Salmaan, pp. 117-118; al-Hilaali, vol. 1, p. 320; Shuaib al-Arnaoot's footnotes to al-Faarisi, vol. 3, pp. 192-193; Bashaar Maroof and Shuaib al-Arnaoot, *Tahreer Taqreeb al-Tahdheeb* (Beirut: Muasassah al-Risaalah, 1997), vol. 3, p. 441.—JZ

[2] Ibn al-Qayyim mentions forty-one different times or occasion in which it is either obligatory or recommend to pray for the Prophet (peace be upon him). [See ibn al-Qayyim, pp. 463-611.] Some of those stated times may be based on hadith which are not acceptable.—JZ

[3] Ibn al-Qayyim discusses the cases of saying prayers for the Prophet (peace be upon him) as (1) before the supplication and after praising Allah, (2) at the beginning, middle and end of the supplication and (3) at the beginning and end of the supplication. See ibn al-Qayyim, *Jalaa*, pp. 531ff. Some of the hadith related to these three categories do reach the level of *hasan*.—JZ

(2) When mentioning him. (Recorded by al-Tirmidhi.[1])

(3) During the night and day of Friday. (Recorded by Abu Dawood.[2])

(4) In every gathering. (Recorded by Ahmad.) And on other occasions [one should state prayers for the Prophet (peace be upon him)].

(5) Reciting the Quran

(1) Al-Nawawi wrote in his book *al-Adhkaar*, "Know that the reciting of the Quran is the most stressed of the words of remembrance. One must read it continuously and not pass any day or night without reading it."

(2) The Messenger of Allah (peace be upon him) said,

اقْرَءُوا الْقُرْآنَ فَإِنَّهُ يَأْتِي يَوْمَ الْقِيَامَةِ شَفِيعًا لِأَصْحَابِهِ اقْرَءُوا الزَّهْرَاوَيْنِ

الْبَقَرَةَ وَسُورَةَ آلِ عِمْرَانَ...

"Read the Quran, for it will come as an intercessor for its companion. Read [in particular] the two flowers: *al-Baqara* and *ali-Imraan..* " (Recorded by Muslim.)

(3) It is recommended to read *soorah al-Baqara* [in particular]. This is because of the hadith,

إِنَّ الشَّيْطَانَ يَنْفِرُ مِنَ الْبَيْتِ الَّذِي تُقْرَأُ فِيهِ سُورَةُ الْبَقَرَة

"Certainly, Satan flees from the house in which *soorah al-Baqara* is recited." (Recorded by Muslim.)

(4) It is recommended to read *soorah al-Kahf* on Fridays, based on the hadith,

من قرأ سورة الكهف يوم الجمعة أوضاء له من النور ما بين الجمعتين

---

[1] Many hadith may be quoted to substantiate this aspect. In particular, one of the hadith recorded by al-Tirmidhi is *hasan*. See ibn al-Qayyim, *Jalaa*, p. 542.

[2] For the relevant hadith on this point, see ibn al-Qayyim, *Jalaa*, pp. 570f.

"Whoever reads *soorah al-Kahf* on Friday will have a light for him between the two Fridays." (Recorded by al-Haakim. This hadith has been narrated through different chains which support each other. They, taken as a whole, indicate that it is sanctioned to recite *soorah al-Kahf* on Fridays.)

(5) It is recommended to memorize the first ten verses of *soorah al-Kahf* because the Prophet (peace be upon him) said,

مَنْ حَفِظَ عَشْرَ آيَاتٍ مِنْ أَوَّلِ سُورَةِ الْكَهْفِ عُصِمَ مِنَ الدَّجَّالِ

"The one who memorizes the first ten verses of *soorah al-Kahf* will be protected from the anti-Christ." (Recorded by Muslim.)

(6) It is recommended to recite *soorah al-Mulk*, based on the hadith,

إِنَّ سُورَةً مِنَ الْقُرْآنِ ثَلَاثُونَ آيَةً شَفَعَتْ لِرَجُلٍ حَتَّى غُفِرَ لَهُ وَهِيَ سُورَةُ
تَبَارَكَ الَّذِي بِيَدِهِ الْمُلْكُ

"There is a *soorah* of the Quran that consists of thirty verses and it interceded for a man until he was forgiven because of it. It is the *soorah* [that begins], 'Blessed be the One in whose Hand is the Dominion.'" (Recorded by al-Tirmidhi and al-Haakim.[1])

(7) It is recommended that when one finishes reading *soorah al-Qiyaamah*, one says, "Certainly, and I am a witness to that, we believe in Allah." When the person finishes *soorah al-Mursalaat*, he should say, "We have believed in Allah." And at the finish of *soorah al-Teen*, one should say, "Certainly, and to that I am one of the witnesses." (Recorded by Abu Dawood.[2])

(8) It is recommended for one to beautify his voice upon reading the Quran. This is based on the Prophet's statement,

---

[1] According to al-Albani, this hadith is *hasan*. See al-Albani, *Sahih al-Jaami*, vol. 1, pp. 420-421.

[2] According to al-Albani, this hadith is weak. See al-Albani, *Dhaeef al-Jaami*, p. 834.

مَا أَذِنَ اللَّهُ لِشَيْءٍ مَا أَذِنَ لِنَبِيٍّ حَسَنِ الصَّوْتِ بِالْقُرْآنِ يَجْهَرُ بِهِ

"Allah does not listen to anything as He listens to the recitation of the Quran by a prophet who recites it in an attractive audible sweet sounding voice." (Recorded by al-Bukhari and Muslim.)

(9) It is recommended for a person to supplicate upon finishing a complete reading of the Quran. There is no particular supplication that needs to be said. Instead, the Muslim may make any supplication that is easy for him.

(6) Words of Remembrance for the Time of Going to Sleep

(1) It is recommended to make ablution before going to one's bed, to wipe the bed before getting into to it, to bring together one's palms and lightly spit some mist into them and then recite *soorah al-Ikhlaas* (number 112, "Say: He is Allah Alone), *soorah al-Falaq* (number 113, "Say: I seek refuge in the Lord of the Daybreak") and *soorah al-Naas* (number 114, "Say: I seek refuge in the Lord of mankind"). After doing so, the person should wipe over as much of his body as he can, beginning with his head and face. He should do that three times. (Recorded by al-Bukhari.)

(2) One should read the "Verse of the Throne," "Allah, there is none worthy of worship but Him, the All-Living, the Sustainer.." [al-Baqara 255]. (Recorded by al-Bukhari.)

(3) One should say, "Exalted and perfected is Allah[1]," thirty-three times, "All praises are to Allah[2]," thirty-three times, and, "Allah is the greatest[3]," thirty-four times. This is based on the hadith of Ali in which the Prophet (peace

---

[1] *Dhikr* #14: *Subhaanallah.*
[2] *Dhikr* #15: *Al-hamdulilaah.*
[3] *Dhikr* #16: *Allaahu eakbar.*

be upon him) told him and Faatimah [after they had asked for a servant],

أَلاَ أُعَلِّمُكُمَا خَيْرًا مِمَّا سَأَلْتُمَانِي إِذَا أَخَذْتُمَا مَضَاجِعَكُمَا تُكَبِّرَا أَرْبَعًا

وَثَلاثِينَ وَتُسَبِّحَا ثَلاثًا وَثَلاثِينَ وَتَحْمَدَا ثَلاثًا وَثَلاثِينَ فَهُوَ خَيْرٌ لَكُمَا

مِنْ خَادِمٍ

"Let me tell what is better than what you asked for. When you go to your beds, extol Allah's greatness thirty-four times, extol His perfection thirty-three times and praise Him thirty-three times. That is better for you than a servant." (Recorded by al-Bukhari.)

(4) Then the person should lay on his right side and say,

بِاسْمِكَ رَبِّ وَضَعْتُ جَنْبِي وَبِكَ أَرْفَعُهُ إِنْ أَمْسَكْتَ نَفْسِي فَارْحَمْهَا

وَإِنْ أَرْسَلْتَهَا فَاحْفَظْهَا بِمَا تَحْفَظُ بِهِ عِبَادَكَ الصَّالِحِينَ

"In Your name my Lord do I lay myself on my side and by You I rise. If You keep my soul, then show it mercy. If You return it [to live longer], then protect it in the manner that You protect Your righteous servants.[1]" He should also say,

اللَّهُمَّ أَسْلَمْتُ نَفْسِي إِلَيْكَ وَفَوَّضْتُ أَمْرِي إِلَيْكَ وَأَلْجَأْتُ ظَهْرِي إِلَيْكَ

رَهْبَةً وَرَغْبَةً إِلَيْكَ لا مَلْجَأَ وَلا مَنْجَا مِنْكَ إِلاَّ إِلَيْكَ آمَنْتُ بِكِتَابِكَ

الَّذِي أَنْزَلْتَ وَبِنَبِيِّكَ الَّذِي أَرْسَلْتَ

"O Allah, I have submitted my soul to You and have entrusted my affairs to You. I also rely upon You, with hope and fear in You. There is no escape or refuge from You except to You. I

---

[1] *Dhikr* #17: *Bismika rabbi wada'tu janbee wa bika ₡arfa'uhu ₡in ₡amsakta nafsee farḥabmhaa wa ₡in ₡arsaltahaa faḥfaDHbaa bimaa taḥfaDHu bibi 'ibaadaka-saaliheen.*

have believed in Your book that You revealed and Your prophet that You sent.[1]" (Recorded by al-Bukhari.)

(5) When one wakes from his sleep, he should say,

الْحَمْدُ لِلَّهِ الَّذِي أَحْيَانَا بَعْدَ مَا أَمَاتَنَا وَإِلَيْهِ النُّشُورُ

"All praise be to Allah who gave us life after He had given us death and to Him is the return.[2]" (Recorded by al-Bukhari.) One also says,

الْحَمْدُ لله الَّذِي رَدَّ عَلَيَّ رُوْحِي وَعَافَانِي فِي جَسَدِي وَأَذِنَ لِي بِذِكْرِه

"All praise be to Allah, the One who returned to me my soul, gave me health in my body and permitted me to remember Him.[3]" (Recorded by ibn al-Sunee.[4])

(6) If someone is troubled by insomnia[5], it is narrated that he should say,

اللهم غارت النجوم وهدأت العيون وأنت حي قيوم لا تأخذك سنة

ولا نوم يا حي يا قيوم أهدىء ليلي وأنم عيني

---

[1] *Dhikr* #18: *Allahumma ṣaslamtu nafsee ṣilaika wa fawwadtu ṣamree ṣilaika wa ṣalja ṣtu DHahree ṣilaika rahbatan wa ragbatan ṣilaika, laa malja ṣa wa laa manjaa minka ṣilla ṣilaika, aamantu bikitaabika-lladhee ṣanzalta wa binabiyyaka-lladhee ṣarsalta.*

[2] *Dhikr* #19: *al-hamdulilaahi-lladhee ṣahyaanaa ba'da maa ṣamaatanaa wa ṣilaihi-n-nushoor.*

[3] *Dhikr* #20: *al-hamdulilaahi-lladhee radda 'alayya roohee wa 'aafaanee fi jasadee wa adhina lee bidhikrihi.*

[4] These words may be found in al-Nasaai's *al-Sunan al-Kubraa* and ibn al-Sunee in *'Amal al-Yaum wa al-Lailah.* According to Saalim al-Salafi, the hadith is *sahih.* The same words may also be found in a hadith in *Sunan al-Tirmidhi* which al-Albani has graded *hasan.* See Saalim al-Salafi's footnotes to Ahmad ibn al-Sunee, *Kitaab 'Amal al-Yaum wa al-Lailah* (Beirut: Muasassah al-Kutub al-Thaqaafiyyah, 1988), p. 8; al-Albani, *Sahih al-Jaami,* vol. 1, p. 184.—JZ

[5] It is also authentically reported that one should say the following for insomnia: "I seek refuge in Allah's perfect words from His anger and His punishment, and from the evil of His servants and from the evil prompting of the devils or that they should be in my midst." [These are virtually the same words as found in the following passage above and whose transliteration may be found under "*Dhikr* #21". The additional words here are, "*min 'iqaabihi*" which come after "*gadabihi*".]

"O Allah, the stars have set and the eyes have been made calm, and You are living, sustaining, neither drowsiness or sleep over takes You, O Living One, O Sustaining One, make my night calm and make my eyes sleep." (Recorded by ibn al-Sunee.[1])

(7) If one is startled in his sleep, he should say,

أَعُوذُ بِكَلِمَاتِ اللهِ التَّامَّةِ مِنْ غَضَبِهِ وَشَرِّ عِبَادِهِ وَمِنْ هَمَزَاتِ الشَّيَاطِينِ وَأَنْ يَحْضُرُونِ

"I seek refuge in Allah's perfect words from His anger and the evil of His servants and from the evil prompting of the devils or that they should be in my midst."[2] (Recorded by Abu Dawood.[3])

(8) If the person sees something in his dream that pleases him, he should praise Allah for it. He should only tell those whom he loves about it. If he sees something he dislikes, he should "lightly spit" on his left side and seek refuge from its evil three times. In that case, it will not harm him. He should not mention that disliked aspect to anyone. He should also change his side upon which he was sleeping. (Recorded by Muslim.)

The Prophet (peace be upon him) forbade telling others about how Satan sported with him in his sleep. The Prophet (peace be upon him) stated,

لَا يُحَدِّثَنَّ أَحَدُكُمْ بِتَلَعُّبِ الشَّيْطَانِ بِهِ فِي مَنَامِهِ

---

[1] According to Saalim al-Salafi, this hadith has a weak chain. However, his grading may be somewhat generous. In the chain of the hadith is Muhammad ibn Alaatha. Ibn Hibbaan stated that this Muhammad would narrate fabricated reports on the authority of trustworthy narrators. Furthermore, al-Bukhari said that there is some question about him, which was one of al-Bukhari's harshest terms of criticism. Hence, the chain should be considered very weak and not simply weak. Allah knows best. (See al-Salafi, pp. 261-262.)—JZ

[2] *Dhikr* #21: *ɛa'oodhu bikalimaati-laahi-taammati min gadabihi wa sharri 'ibaadihi wa min hamazaati-shayaateen wa ɛan yahduroon.*

[3] According to al-Albani, this hadith is *hasan*. See al-Albani, *Sahih Sunan Abi Dawood*, vol. 2, p. 737.—JZ

"None of you should ever tell others about how Satan sported
with him during his sleep." (Recorded by Muslim.)

(9) If a person awakes during his sleep and wishes to
change his side upon which he is sleeping, he should say,

لَا إِلَهَ إِلاَّ اللَّهُ وَحْدَهُ لَا شَرِيكَ لَهُ لَهُ الْمُلْكُ وَلَهُ الْحَمْدُ وَهُوَ عَلَى كُلِّ
شَيْءٍ قَدِيرٌ الْحَمْدُ لِلَّهِ وَسُبْحَانَ اللَّهِ وَلَا إِلَهَ إِلاَّ اللَّهُ وَاللَّهُ أَكْبَرُ وَلَا حَوْلَ
وَلَا قُوَّةَ إِلاَّ بِاللَّهِ اللهُمَّ اغْفِرْ لِي

"There is none worthy of worship except Allah, alone who
has no partner with Him. To Him belongs the dominion and to
Him is the praise. He has power over all things. All praises
are due to Allah. Exalted and perfect is Allah. There is none
worthy of worship except Allah. Allah is the Greatest. There is
no movement or might except by Allah. O Allah, forgive
me."[1] This is based on the hadith in *Sahih al-Bukhari* on the
authority of Ibaadah ibn al-Saamit that the Prophet (peace be
upon him) said,

مَنْ تَعَارَّ مِنَ اللَّيْلِ فَقَالَ < لَا إِلَهَ إِلاَّ اللَّهُ وَحْدَهُ لَا شَرِيكَ لَهُ لَهُ الْمُلْكُ
وَلَهُ الْحَمْدُ وَهُوَ عَلَى كُلِّ شَيْءٍ قَدِيرٌ الْحَمْدُ لِلَّهِ وَسُبْحَانَ اللَّهِ وَلَا إِلَهَ
إِلاَّ اللَّهُ وَاللَّهُ أَكْبَرُ وَلَا حَوْلَ وَلَا قُوَّةَ إِلاَّ بِاللَّهِ > ثُمَّ قَالَ اللَّهُمَّ اغْفِرْ لِي
أَوْ دَعَا اسْتُجِيبَ لَهُ فَإِنْ تَوَضَّأَ وَصَلَّى قُبِلَتْ صَلَاتُهُ

"If someone wakes during the night and says, 'There is none
worthy of worship except Allah, alone who has no partner
with Him. To Him belongs the dominion and to Him is the
praise. He has power over all things. All praises are due to
Allah. Exalted and perfect is Allah. There is none worthy of
worship except Allah. Allah is the Greatest. There is no
movement or might except by Allah' and then he says, 'O

---

[1] *Dhikr* #22: *Laa ṣilaaha ṣilla-llaahu waḥdahu laa shareeka lahu lahu-l-
mulku wa lahu-l-ḥamdu wa huwa 'ala kulli shaiṣin qadeerun wa-l-
ḥamdulilaahi wa subḥaanallaahi wa laa ṣilaaha ṣilla-llaahu wallahu ṣakbar
wa laa ḥaula wa laa quwwata ṣilla bi-laahi. Allahumma-gfirlee.*

Allah, forgive me,' or a supplication, he will be responded to. If he makes ablution and prays, his prayers will be accepted."[1]

(10) It is recommended to survey and check the house before one's sleep. Including among the acts one should perform are, as mentioned in the following hadith,

أَطْفِئُوا الْمَصَابِيحَ إِذَا رَقَدْتُمْ وَغَلِّقُوا الأَبْوَابَ وَأَوْكُوا الأَسْقِيَةَ وَخَمِّرُوا الطَّعَامَ وَالشَّرَابَ وَأَحْسِبُهُ قَالَ وَلَوْ بِعُودٍ تَعْرُضُهُ عَلَيْهِ

"Put out the lamps at night when you go to bed; close the doors; tie up the waterskins; and cover the food and drink," and, "I [the subnarrator] think he also said, '[Cover them] even with a stick that is placed over them.'" (Recorded by al-Bukhari.)

The Messenger of Allah (peace be upon him) also said,

إِنَّ هَذِهِ النَّارَ إِنَّمَا هِيَ عَدُوٌّ لَكُمْ فَإِذَا نِمْتُمْ فَأَطْفِئُوهَا عَنْكُمْ

"This fire is certainly an enemy to you. Therefore, when you sleep, put them out to protect yourselves." (Recorded by al-Bukhari.)

(7) Words of Remembrance Said When Entering or Leaving Bathrooms

(1) When a person intends to enter a bathroom, he should say,

اللَّهُمَّ إِنِّي أَعُوذُ بِكَ مِنَ الْخُبُثِ وَالْخَبَائِثِ

---

[1] It is not clear to this translator the relationship between the hadith quoted and the turning from one side to another during one's sleep. This hadith was also recorded by al-Tirmidhi, ibn Majah, Abu Dawood, Ahmad and al-Daarimi. In their narrations also, there is no mention of turning from one side to the other in one's sleep. Allah knows best.—JZ

"O Allah, I seek refuge in You from the male and female devils."[1] (Recorded by al-Bukhari and Muslim.)

(2) If a person intends to remove his clothing, it is sanctioned for him to say what has been narrated on the authority of Ali ibn Abu Taalib that the Prophet (peace be upon him) said,

سَتْرُ مَا بَيْنَ أَعْيُنِ الْجِنِّ وَعَوْرَاتِ بَنِي آدَمَ إِذَا دَخَلَ أَحَدُهُمُ الْخَلَاءَ أَنْ
يَقُولَ < بِسْمِ اللَّهِ >

"The covering between the eyes of the jinn and the private parts of humans when one of them enters the bathroom is for them to say, 'In the name of Allah.'[2]" (Recorded by al-Tirmidhi and others.[3])

(3) Upon leaving the bathroom, one should say,

غُفْرَانَكَ

الْحَمْدُ لِلَّهِ الَّذِي أَذْهَبَ عَنِّي الأَذَى وَعَافَانِي

"[I seek] Your forgiveness.[4] All praise be to Allah who removed from me what is harmful and made me healthy." (Recorded by al-Tirmidhi and ibn Maajah.[5])

(4) It is disliked to speak while relieving oneself. This is based on the hadith in which a man passed by the Prophet

---

1 *Dhikr* #23: *Allaahumma çinnee ça'ood̲h̲u bika min al-k̲h̲ubut̲h̲i wa-l-k̲h̲abaa çith.*

2 *Dhikr* #24: *Bismilaah.*

3 According to al-Albani, this hadith is *sahih*. See al-Albani, *Sahih al-Jaami*, vol. 1, p. 675.—JZ

4 *Dhikr* #25: *Gufraanak.*

5 The manner in which these hadith presented is not proper. The published work makes it look like these statements are all from one hadith. Actually, they are from two separate hadith. The first hadith that only states, "I seek Your forgiveness" has been recorded by al-Tirmidhi, Abu Dawood and ibn Maajah. According to al-Albani, that hadith is *hasan*. See al-Albani, *Sahih al-Jaami*, vol. 2, p. 859. The second hadith, containing the remaining of the words above, was recorded only by ibn Maajah and not by al-Tirmidhi or others. According to al-Albani, this second hadith is weak. See al-Albani, *Dhaeef al-Jaami al-Sagheer*, p. 635.—JZ

(peace be upon him) while he was urinating. The man greeted him but the Prophet (peace be upon him) did not respond. (Recorded by Muslim.)

(8) What is Sanctioned for Before and After Performing Ablution

(1) It is sanctioned for the person to say, "In the name of Allah,[1]" when beginning to perform ablution. If the person forgets it at the beginning, he may say it during the act. He should begin his acts of ablution with the parts on the right side of his body, based on the hadith,

إِذَا لَبِسْتُمْ وَإِذَا تَوَضَّأْتُمْ فَابْدَءُوا بِأَيَامِنِكُمْ

"When you get dressed or make ablution, start with your right side." (Recorded by Abu Dawood.[2])

(2) After finishing the ablution, one should say, as is mentioned in the hadith,

مَنْ تَوَضَّأَ فَقَالَ < أَشْهَدُ أَنْ لا إِلَهَ إِلاَّ اللَّهُ وَحْدَهُ لا شَرِيكَ لَهُ وَأَشْهَدُ
أَنَّ مُحَمَّدًا عَبْدُهُ وَرَسُولُهُ < فُتِحَتْ لَهُ أَبْوَابُ الْجَنَّةِ الثَّمَانِيَةُ يَدْخُلُ مِنْ
أَيِّهَا شَاءَ

"Whoever makes ablution and says, 'I bear witness that there is none worthy of worship except Allah, alone, without any partner with Him. And I bear witness that Muhammad is His servant and messenger,[3]' the eight doors of Paradise will be opened for him and he will be able to enter through any of them he wishes." (Recorded by Muslim and al-Tirmidhi.) [Al-Tirmidhi has] the additional words,

---

[1] *Dhikr* #26: *Bismilaah.*

[2] According to al-Albani, this hadith is *sahih.* See al-Albani, *Sahih al-Jaami*, vol. 1, p. 198.—JZ

[3] *Dhikr* #27: *ashhadu an laa silaaha silla-llaahu wahdahu laa shareeka lahu wa ashhadu sanna muhammadan 'abduhu wa rasooluhu.*

اللَّهُمَّ اجْعَلْنِي مِنَ التَّوَّابِينَ وَاجْعَلْنِي مِنَ الْمُتَطَهِّرِينَ

"O Allah, make me from those who repent often and make me from those who purify themselves.[1]"[2]

(9) Words of Remembrance Related to Clothing and Dressing

(1) It is preferred for one who is dressing to start with his right side. (Recorded by Abu Dawud.[3])

(2) If a person wears a new garment or new footwear, he should say,

اللَّهُمَّ لَكَ الْحَمْدُ أَنْتَ كَسَوْتَنِيهِ أَسْأَلُكَ خَيْرَهُ وَخَيْرَ مَا صُنِعَ لَهُ وَأَعُوذُ
بِكَ مِنْ شَرِّهِ وَشَرِّ مَا صُنِعَ لَهُ

"O Allah to You is the praise. You are the one who clothed me with it. I ask of You for its good and the good that it was made for. And I seek refuge in You from its evil and the evil that it was made for.[4]" (Recorded by Abu Dawood and al-Tirmidhi.[5])

(3) If a person sees another person wearing a new garment, he should say to him,

تُبْلَى وَيُخْلِفُ اللَّهُ تَعَالَى

---

[1] *Dhikr #28: Allahumma-j'alnee min at-tawwaabeena wa-j'alnee min al-mutatahhireen.*

[2] According to al-Albani, this narration is also *sahih*. See al-Albani, *Sahih al-Jaami*, vol. 2, p. 1061.—JZ

[3] This was mentioned earlier and is based on an authentic hadith.—JZ

[4] *Dhikr #29: Allaahumma laka-l-hamdu ɛanta kisautineehi ɛasɛaluka khairahu wa khaira maa suni'a lahu wa ɛa'oodhu bika min sharrihi wa sharri maa suni'a lahu.*

[5] According to al-Albani, this hadith is *sahih*. See al-Albani, *Sahih al-Jaami*, vol. 2, p. 853. It should be noted that some of the other narrations of this hadith have a very slight difference in the wording.—JZ

"May you wear it out and may Allah, Most High, replace it [with another].¹" (Recorded by Abu Dawood.²)

(4) When a person is going to take off his clothing, he should say,

بِسْمِ اللهِ الَّذِي لا إِلهَ إِلا هُو

"In the name of Allah, besides whom there is none worthy of worship." It is authentically narrated from the Prophet (peace be upon him) that the covering between the eyes of the jinn and the private part of humans is for the servant to say, "In the name of Allah, besides whom there is none worthy of worship." (Recorded by ibn al-Sunee and others.³)

(10) Words of Remembrance Related to Entering or Leave the House

(1) When entering one's house, one should say,

اللّهُمَّ إِنِّي أَسْأَلُكَ خَيْرَ الْمَوْلَجِ وَخَيْرَ الْمَخْرَجِ بِسْمِ اللّهِ وَلَجْنَا وَبِسْمِ
اللّهِ خَرَجْنَا وَعَلَى اللّهِ رَبِّنَا تَوَكَّلْنَا

"O Allah, I ask You for the best entering and the best exiting. In the name of Allah I enter and in the name of Allah I leave and upon Allah, our Lord, do we put our trust." Then he should greet his family for it is blessings upon him and upon them. (Recorded by Abu Dawood and al-Tirmidhi.⁴)

---

¹ *Dhikr* #30: *tublaa wa yukhlifu-llaahu ta'alaa.*

² According to al-Albani, the related hadith is *sahih*. See al-Albani, *Sahih Sunan Abi Dawood*, vol. 2, p. 760.—JZ

³ According to al-Salafi, this hadith is very weak. Indeed, the only authentic hadith related to this topic are those which only mention the words, "In the name of Allah," without any additional words to the supplication. See al-Salafi, p. 100; al-Albani, *Sahih al-Jaami*, vol. 1, p. 675.—JZ

⁴ First, this hadith was recorded by Abu Dawood and al-Tabaraani; it seems that al-Tirmidhi has not narrated this hadith at all. It is possible that such was a typographical error. Second, this hadith is a weak hadith, as al-Hilaali has demonstrated. He further points out that this is a hadith that al-Albani used to

(2) Upon leaving one's house, one should say,

بِسْمِ اللَّهِ تَوَكَّلْتُ عَلَى اللَّهِ لا حَوْلَ وَلا قُوَّةَ إِلاَّ بِاللَّهِ

اللَّهُمَّ إِنِي أَعُوذُ بِكَ أَنْ أَضِلَّ أَوْ أُضَلَّ أَوْ أَزِلَّ أَوْ أُزَلَّ أَوْ أَظْلِمَ أَوْ أُظْلَمَ

أَوْ أَجْهَلَ أَوْ يُجْهَلَ عَلَيَّ

"In the name of Allah. I put my trust in Allah. There is no
movement or power except in Allah.[1] O Allah, I seek refuge
in You from going astray or being led astray, from slipping or
being made to slip, from wronging others or having wrong
done to me, from acting in ignorance or being acted toward
in ignorance.[2]" (Recorded by Abu Dawood.[3])

(3) It is recommended for the person to eat seven
ajwah dates[4] in the morning, based on the hadith,

مَنْ تَصَبَّحَ كُلَّ يَوْمٍ سَبْعَ تَمَرَاتٍ عَجْوَةً لَمْ يَضُرُّهُ فِي ذَلِكَ الْيَوْمِ سُمٌّ وَلا

سِحْرٌ

"Whoever eats seven *ajwah* dates every morning will not be
harmed on that day by any poison or magic." (Recorded by
al-Bukhari.)

---

consider authentic and then he later changed his opinion about it. See al-Hilaali,
vol. 1, p. 102.—JZ

[1] *Dhikr* #31: *bismilaahi tawakkaltu 'ala-llaahi laa haula wa laa quwwata
eilla bi-laah.*

[2] *Dhikr* #32: *Allaahumma einnee ea'oodhu bika ean eadilla eau eudalla
eau eazilla eau euzalla eau eaDHlim eau euDHlama eau eajhala eau
yujhala 'alayya.*

[3] In this case, the author has combined together two separate hadith that may both
be found in *Sunan Abu Dawood* and other works. Both hadith are authentic. See
al-Hilaali, vol. 1, p. 99.—JZ

[4] These are a type of date found in Madeenah.

(11) Words of Remembrance Related to the Call to Prayer

(1) When the person hears the one making the call to prayer, he should repeat after him, except when he says, "*Hayya ala-salaah*," and "*Hayya ala-l-falaah*." After hearing those expressions, the person should say,

لا حَوْلَ وَلا قُوَّةَ إلاَّ بِاللَّهِ

"There is no movement or might except in Allah.[1]" [The Prophet (peace be upon him) said about all of those words,]

مَنْ قَالَ ذَلِكَ مِنْ قَلْبِهِ دَخَلَ الْجَنَّةَ

"Whoever says that from his heart will enter Paradise." Then he should pray for the Prophet (peace be upon him). (Recorded by Muslim.)

(2) The person should ask Allah to grant the Prophet Muhammad (peace be upon him) the position of *al-waseelah*[2] (a rank in Paradise), as is stated in the following hadith,

مَنْ قَالَ حِينَ يَسْمَعُ النِّدَاءَ < اللَّهُمَّ رَبَّ هَذِهِ الدَّعْوَةِ التَّامَّةِ وَالصَّلاةِ

الْقَائِمَةِ آتِ مُحَمَّدًا الْوَسِيلَةَ وَالْفَضِيلَةَ وَابْعَثْهُ مَقَامًا مَحْمُودًا الَّذِي

وَعَدْتَهُ > حَلَّتْ لَهُ شَفَاعَتِي يَوْمَ الْقِيَامَةِ

"Whoever says upon hearing the call to prayer, 'O Allah, Lord of this perfect call[3] and the prayer about to be performed, grant Muhammad *al-waseelah* and *al-fadheelah*[4], and resurrect him to the praiseworthy position

---

[1] *Dhikr #33: Laa haula wa laa quwwata ɛilla bilaah.*

[2] A narration in *Sahih Muslim* states that this is a rank in Paradise that is only becoming a devoted servant of Allah.—JZ

[3] This is in reference to the call of *tauheed* and the belief in the Prophet Muhammad (peace be upon him).—JZ

[4] This is a position that is greater than the rest of creation or it could be considered a kind of description of the place of *al-waseelah*. Allah knows best.—JZ

that You had promised him,[1]' will be granted my intercession on the Day of Resurrection." (Recorded by al-Bukhari.)

(3) Supplication after the call to prayer is responded to. The Prophet (peace be upon him) has said,

الدُّعَاءُ لا يُرَدُّ بَيْنَ الأَذَانِ وَالإِقَامَةِ قَالُوا فَمَاذَا نَقُولُ يَا رَسُولَ اللّهِ قَالَ

سَلُوا اللّهَ الْعَافِيَةَ فِي الدُّنْيَا وَالْآخِرَة

"The supplication between the call to prayer and the *iqaamah*[2] is not rejected." They said, "What shall we say, o Messenger of Allah (peace be upon him)?" He replied, "Ask Allah for well-being in this life and in the Hereafter." (Recorded by al-Tirmidhi.[3])

Also at the time that the prayer is being commenced, one should supplicate to Allah. The Prophet (peace be upon him) said,

ساعتان لا ترد على داع دعوته حين تقام الصلاة وفي الصف في سبيل

الله

"There are two times in which the supplication of the supplicant is not rejected: when the prayer is being

---

[1] *Dhikr #34: Allahumma rabba hadhihi-da'wati-ttaammati wa-ssalaati-l-qaa ¢imati aati muhammadan al-waseelah wa-l-fadeelata wab'athhu maqaaman mahmoodan alladhee wa'adtahu.*

[2] The *iqaamah* is the call to prayer that is stated just before the prayer begins and signifies that the prayer is actually beginning.—JZ

[3] The portion of the hadith stating that one should supplicate between the call to prayer and the *iqaamah* is supported by a strong hadith in *Musnad Ahmad* and elsewhere. However, the portion, quoted above, from the hadith in *Sunan al-Tirmidhi* that states what one should say is rejected. It has been declared weak or rejected by al-Hilaali, Abdul Qaadir al-Arnaoot and al-Albani. There is nothing wrong with the supplication itself, as it has been mentioned in other authentic hadith but there is no support for it, in particular, at the time mentioned in this hadith. See al-Hilaali, vol. 1, p. 136; Abdul Qaadir al-Arnaoot's footnotes to al-Mubaarak ibn al-Atheer, *Jaami al-Usool fi Ahadeeth al-Rasool* (Maktabah al-Halwaani, 1970), vol. 4, p. 142.—JZ

commenced and in the ranks [while battling] for the sake of Allah." (Recorded by al-Haakim.[1])

(12) Words of Remembrance Related to the Mosque

(1) It is recommended for one to leave early for the mosque and to sit in the first row. This is based on the Prophet's statement,

$$لَوْ يَعْلَمُ النَّاسُ مَا فِي النِّدَاءِ وَالصَّفِّ الْأَوَّلِ ثُمَّ لَمْ يَجِدُوا إِلَّا أَنْ يَسْتَهِمُوا عَلَيْهِ لَاَسْتَهَمُوا$$

"If the people knew what [virtues] lie in the call to prayer and the first row and they had no way to [determine who would get them] except through drawing lots, they would certainly draw lots." (Recorded by al-Bukhari.)

(2) Upon entering the mosque, the person should begin with his right foot and say[2],

$$بِسْمِ اللهِ اللَّهُمَّ صَلِّ عَلَى مُحَمَّدٍ$$

$$رَبِّ اغْفِرْ لِي ذُنُوبِي وَافْتَحْ لِي أَبْوَابَ رَحْمَتِكَ$$

$$أَعُوذُ بِاللهِ الْعَظِيمِ وَبِوَجْهِهِ الْكَرِيمِ وَسُلْطَانِهِ الْقَدِيمِ مِنَ الشَّيْطَانِ الرَّجِيمِ$$

"In the name of Allah. O Allah, shower blessings upon Muhammad.[3] My Lord, forgive me my sins and open for me

---

1 Al-Nawawi and al-Hilaali have declared a hadith similar to this one authentic. See al-Hilaali, vol. 1, p. 136.—JZ

2 Unfortunately, in this paragraph and the following, the author has combined together a number of hadith and simply stated that it was recorded by different authorities. The purpose of the author is to keep things simple for the masses. However, this is not an acceptable way to ascribe hadith. Hence, each shall be discussed separately below.—JZ

3 *Dhikr* #35: *bismilaahi allahumma salli 'ala muhammad*. This has been recorded by ibn al-Sunee. It has some weakness in its chain but due to supporting evidence, it is considered *hasan*. See al-Hilaali, vol. 1, p. 121.

the doors of Your mercy.[1] I seek refuge in Allah, the Great, and in His Noble Face and ancient rule, from the accursed Satan.[2]" (Recorded by Muslim, Abu Dawood, al-Tirmidhi and al-Baihaqi.)

(3) Upon leaving the mosque, the person should begin with his left foot and say,

بِسْمِ اللهِ اللَّهُمَّ صَلِّ عَلَى مُحَمَّدٍ

رَبِّ اغْفِرْ لِي ذُنُوبِي وَافْتَحْ لِي أَبْوَابَ فَضْلِكَ

اللَّهُمَّ اعْصِمْنِي مِنَ الشَّيْطَانِ الرَّجِيم

"In the name of Allah. O Allah, shower blessings upon Muhammad.[3] My Lord, forgive me my sins and open for me the doors of Your grace.[4] O Allah, protect me from Satan, the accursed.[5]"

(4) Anyone who is buying or selling in the mosque or announcing the fact that he lost something should be stopped or rebuked. A hadith states,

إِذَا رَأَيْتُمْ مَنْ يَبِيعُ أَوْ يَبْتَاعُ فِي الْمَسْجِدِ فَقُولُوا لا أَرْبَحَ اللَّهُ تِجَارَتَكَ

وَإِذَا رَأَيْتُمْ مَنْ يَنْشُدُ فِيهِ ضَالَّةً فَقُولُوا لا رَدَّ اللَّهُ عَلَيْكَ

---

[1] *Dhikr* #36: *rabbi-gfirlee lee dhunoobee wa-ftah lee ḍabwaaba rahmatik*. With this wording, the hadith was recorded by al-Tirmidhi. According to al-Albani, it is *sahih*. See Muhammad Nasir al-Deen al-Albani, *Sahih Sunan al-Tirmidhi* (Riyadh: Maktab al-Tarbiyyah al-Arabi li-Duwal al-Khaleej, 1988), vol. 1, pp. 101-102.

[2] *Dhikr* #37: *ḍa'oodhu bilaahi-l-'aDHeemi wa biwajhihi-l-kareem wa sultaanihi-l-qadeemi mina-shaitaani-rajeem*. This hadith was recorded by Abu Dawood. It has been declared authentic by al-Hilaali. See al-Hilaali, vol. 1, p. 121.

[3] This is the same as *Dhikr* #35. It is considered *hasan*. See al-Hilaali, vol. 1, p. 121.

[4] *Dhikr* #38: *rabbi-gfirlee lee dhunoobi wa-ftah lee ḍabwaab fadlik*. With this wording, the hadith was recorded by al-Tirmidhi. According to al-Albani, it is *sahih*. See al-Albani, *Sahih Sunan al-Tirmidhi*, vol. 1, pp. 101-102.—JZ

[5] *Dhikr* #39: *allahumma-'simnee mina-shaitaani-rajeem*. This hadith was recorded by ibn Maajah. According to al-Albani, it is *sahih*. See Muhammad Nasir al-Deen al-Albani, *Sahih Sunan ibn Maajah* (Riyadh: Maktab al-Tarbiyyah al-Arabi li-Duwal al-Khaleej, 1986), vol. 1, p. 129.—JZ

"If you see one selling or buying in the mosque, say, 'May Allah not give you any profit in your business dealing.' And if you see anyone announcing something he has lost, say, 'May Allah not return it to you.'" (Recorded by al-Tirmidhi.[1])

(12) Words of Remembrance for After the Ritual Prayers

(1) After every [obligatory] prayer, one should say,

أَسْتَغْفِرُ اللهَ

"I seek Allah's forgiveness[2]," three times. [And then say,]

اللَّهُمَّ أَنْتَ السَّلامُ وَمِنْكَ السَّلامُ تَبَارَكْتَ يَا ذَا الْجَلالِ وَالْإِكْرَام

"O Allah, You are the One who is free from any shortcoming or vice and from You comes peace. Blessed You are, O One of Grandeur and Honor.[3][4]"

لا إِلهَ إِلاَّ اللهُ وَحْدَهُ لا شَرِيْكَ لَهُ لَهُ الْمُلْكُ وَلَهُ الْحَمْدُ وَهُوَ عَلَى كُلِّ

شَيْءٍ قَدِيْرٌ اللَّهُمَّ لاَ مَانِعَ لِمَا أَعْطَيْتَ وَلاَ مُعْطِيَ لِمَا مَنَعْتَ وَلاَ يَنْفَعُ ذَا

الْجَدِّ مِنْكَ الْجَدُّ

"There is none worthy of worship except Allah, alone, without any partner, to Him is the dominion and to Him is the praise. And He has power over all things. O Allah, there is none who can prevent what You have given. And there is none who can give when You have prevented it. And no owner of

---

[1] According to al-Albani, this hadith is *sahih*. See al-Albani, *Sahih al-Jaami*, vol. 1, p. 160.—JZ

[2] *Dhikr* #40: *astagfirullaah.*

[3] *Dhikr* #41: *Allaahumma ¢anta-salaamu wa minka-salaamu tabaarakta yaa dhaa-l-jalaali wa-l- ¢ikraam.*

[4] This has been recorded by Muslim.—JZ

wealth will be benefited [against You] as all wealth is from You.1"2

[One should also say] each of the following phrases thirty-three times,

سُبْحَانَ الله

"Perfect and extolled is Allah.3"

الْحَمْدُ لِلَّه

"All praise is due Allah.4"

الله أَكْبَر

"Allah is greatest.5"

Then, to complete one hundred statements, one should say,

لا إِلَهَ إِلاَّ اللهُ وَحْدَهُ لا شَرِيْكَ لَهُ لَهُ الْمُلْكُ وَلَهُ الْحَمْدُ وَهُوَ عَلَى كُلِّ
شَيْءٍ قَدِيْرٌ

"There is none worthy of worship except Allah, alone, without any partner, to Him is the dominion and to Him is the praise. And He has power over all things.6" (Recorded by Muslim.)

(2) One should also say,

اللَّهُمَّ أَعِنِّي عَلَى ذِكْرِكَ وَشُكْرِكَ وَحُسْنِ عِبَادَتِكَ

---

1 *Dhikr* #42: *laa ɛilaaha ɛilla-llaah wahdahu laa shareeka lahu lahu-l-mulk wa lahu-l-hamd wa huwa 'ala kulli shai ɛin qadeer. Allaahumma laa mani'a lima ɛa'taita wa laa mu'tiya lima mana'ta wa la yanfa'u dha-l-jaddi minka-l-jadd.*

2 This has been recorded by al-Bukhari and Muslim.—JZ

3 *Dhikr* #43: *subhaanallaah.*

4 *Dhikr* #44: *al-hamdulilaah.*

5 *Dhikr* #45: *Allaahu ɛakbar.*

6 *Dhikr* #46: *laa ɛilaaha ɛilla-llaahu wahdahu laa shareeka lahu lahu-l-mulku wa lahu-l-hamdu wa huwa 'ala kulli shai ɛin qadeer.*

"O Allah, help me in establishing Your remembrance, giving You thanks and excelling in worship of You." (Recorded by Abu Dawood.[1])

(3) After the Morning and Evening Prayer, one should say the following ten times,

لَا إِلَهَ إِلَّا اللهُ وَحْدَهُ لَا شَرِيْكَ لَهُ لَهُ الْمُلْكُ وَلَهُ الْحَمْدُ يُحْيِيْ وَيُمِيْتُ وَهُوَ عَلَى كُلِّ شَيْءٍ قَدِيْرٌ

"There is none worthy of worship except Allah, alone, without any partner, to Him is the dominion and to Him is the praise. He gives life and He brings about death. And He has power over all things.[2]" (Recorded by al-Tirmidhi.[3])

(4) One also says, seven times, after those two prayers,

---

[1] This hadith was recorded by al-Nasaai, Abu Dawood and Ahmad. All of them have recorded this hadith through the same sources. However, in the narration from Abu Dawood and one narration in Ahmad, the reference to when this supplication is to be made is unclear. In the narration in al-Nasaai and one narration in Ahmad, it is explicitly clear that the Prophet (peace be upon him) told Muadh to say those words in his actual ritual prayer and not after the ritual prayer. The vague narrations must be interpreted in light of the clear narrations, especially when their source is one. Therefore, these words should actually be said at the end of the prayer and not as words to be said after one finishes the prayer. Allah knows best. The narration in *Sunan al-Nasaai* is graded *sahih* by al-Albani. See Muhammad Nasir al-Deen al-Albani, *Sahih Sunan al-Nasaai* (Riyadh: Maktab al-Tarbiyyah al-Arabi li-Duwal al-Khaleej, 1988), vol. 1, p. 280. —JZ

[2] *Dhikr #47: laa ṣilaaha ṣilla-llaahu waḥdahu laa shareeka lahu lahu-l-mulku wa lahu-l-ḥamdu yuḥyee wa yumeet wa huwa 'ala kulli shaiṣin qadeer.*

[3] In reality, the hadith about making this statement after the Morning Prayer and after the Evening Prayer are two different hadith. However, both hadith are recorded by al-Tirmidhi. Concerning saying these words after the morning prayer, al-Hilaali has noted a number of problems with the chain of the hadith but concludes that the hadith is *hasan* due to supporting evidence. (See al-Hilaali, vol. 1, pp. 214-215.) The hadith concerning the Evening Prayer has also been graded *hasan* by al-Albani (although he had previously considered it weak). See Muhammad Nasir al-Deen al-Albani, *Sahih al-Targheeb wa al-Tarheeb* (Riyadh: Maktabah al-Maarif, 1988), vol. 1, p. 262.—JZ

اللّٰهُمَّ أَجِرْنِي مِنَ النَّارِ

"O Allah, rescue me from the Fire." If one says that and then dies on that day or night, it will be written for him that he will be distanced from the Hell-fire. (Recorded by Abu Dawood.[1])

(5) One should recite, "the Verse of the Throne" (al-Baqara 255) [after every obligatory prayer] due to the hadith,

من قرأ آية الكرسي دبر كل صلاة مكتوبة لم يحل بينه وبين دخول

الجنة إلا الموت

"For whoever recites the Verse of the Throne after every obligatory prayer there will be no barrier between him and entering Paradise except death." (Recorded by ibn al-Sunee.[2])

(6) One should also read soorah al-Ikhlaas (the 112th soorah) as well as the two soorahs of seeking protection (the 113th and 114th soorahs of the Quran). These are to be read once. (Recorded by Abu Dawood.[3]) However, after the Morning and the Evening Prayers, they should be read three times. (Recorded by al-Tirmidhi.[4])

(7) After saying the salaam after the Witr Prayer, one should say the following three times, making the last statement longest,

سُبْحَانَ الْمَلِكِ الْقُدُّوسِ

---

[1] This hadith was recorded by Ahmad, Abu Dawood and others. It has been declared weak by al-Albani. See al-Albani, Dhaeef al-Jaami, pp. 81-82.—JZ

[2] Recorded by ibn al-Sunee and by al-Nasaai in Sunan al-Kubra and Amal al-Yaum wa al-Lailah. According to al-Albani, it is sahih. See al-Albani, Sahih al-Jaami, vol. 2, p. 1103.—JZ

[3] According to al-Hilaali, this hadith is sahih. See al-Hilaali, vol. 1, pp. 205-206.—JZ

[4] The hadith in al-Tirmidhi simply states that one should say these words three times in the morning and three times in the late afternoon. There is nothing explicit in the hadith about saying these words three times after those specific prayers. That hadith is, incidentally, hasan. See al-Hilaali, vol. 1, p. 220.—JZ

"Perfect is the King, the Holy One.[1]" (Recorded by al-Nasaai.[2])

(8) After the *sunnah* prayer for the Morning Prayer, one should say thrice,

اللهم رب جبريل وإسرافيل وميكائيل ومحمد أعوذ بك من النار

"O Allah, Lord of Gabriel, Israafeel, Michaeel and Muhammad, I seek refuge in You from the Fire." (Recorded by ibn al-Sunee.[3])

(14) Words of Remembrance Related to the Fast

(1) The Prophet (peace be upon him) said,

الصِّيَامُ جُنَّةٌ فَلا يَرْفُثْ وَلا يَجْهَلْ وَإِن امْرُؤٌ قَاتَلَهُ أَوْ شَاتَمَهُ فَلْيَقُلْ إِنِّي صَائِمٌ إِنِّي صَائِمٌ

"Fasting is a shield [from the Hell-fire]. [If one of you is fasting] let him not have foul speech or behave foolishly. If anyone fights with him or abuses him, he should say, 'I am fasting, I am fasting.'" (Recorded by al-Bukhari.)

(2) When the person breaks his fast, he should say,

ذَهَبَ الظَّمَأُ وَابْتَلَّتِ الْعُرُوقُ وَثَبَتَ الأَجْرُ إِنْ شَاءَ اللَّهُ

"The thirst has gone, the veins have become moist and the reward is confirmed, Allah willing.[4]"[1] And he should also say,

---

[1] *Dhikr* #48: *subhaana-l-maliki-l-quddoos.*

[2] According to al-Albani, this hadith is *sahih.* See al-Albani, *Sahih Sunan al-Nasaai,* vol. 1, p. 381.—JZ

[3] This hadith is recorded by ibn al-Sunee, al-Haakim and al-Tabaraani. There is no question that its chain is weak; in fact, it is very weak, as al-Hilaali has noted. See al-Hilaali, vol. 1, p. 137.—JZ

[4] *Dhikr* #49: *dhahaba-DHamaʕu wabtallati-l-ʕurooqu wa thabata-l-ajru ʕinsha ʕallaah.*

اللَّهُمَّ لَكَ صُمْتُ وَعَلَى رِزْقِكَ أَفْطَرْتُ

"O Allah, for You I have fasted and with sustenance from You do I break my fast." (Recorded by Abu Dawood.[2])

(3) If a person breaks his fast with food given to him by others, he should make the following supplication for them,

أَفْطَرَ عِنْدَكُمُ الصَّائِمُونَ وَأَكَلَ طَعَامَكُمُ الْأَبْرَارُ وَصَلَّتْ عَلَيْكُمُ الْمَلَائِكَةُ

"May those who are fasting break their fast with you, and may the pious eat of your food and may the angels invoke blessings for you.[3]" (Recorded by Abu Dawood.[4])

(4) If the person happens to catch the "Night of Decree" (*Lailatul-Qadar*), he should make the following supplication,

اللَّهُمَّ إِنَّكَ عَفُوٌّ تُحِبُّ الْعَفْوَ فَاعْفُ عَنِّي

"O Allah, You are the One who Pardons and You love pardoning, so pardon me.[5]" (Recorded by al-Tirmidhi.[6])

---

[1] This hadith was recorded by Abu Dawood, al-Nasaai in *al-Kubra*, ibn al-Sunee and others. It has been declared *hasan* by scholars such as al-Hilaali. See al-Hilaali, vol. 1, p. 493.—JZ

[2] This hadith has a weak chain. See al-Hilaali, vol. 1, p. 495.—JZ

[3] *Dhikr* #50: *eaftara 'indakumu-ssa eimoona wa eakala ta'aamakumu-l-eabraaru wa sallat 'alaikumu-l-malaa eikah.*

[4] According to al-Hilaali and others, this hadith is *sahih*. See, for example, al-Hilaali, vol. 1, p. 497.—JZ

[5] *Dhikr* #51: *Allaahumma einnaka 'afuwwun tuhibbu-l-'afwa fa'fu 'annee.*

[6] According to al-Hilaali, this hadith is *sahih*. See al-Hilaali, vol. 1, p. 497.

(15) Words of Remembrance for Specific Occasions or Times that Arise

(1) *Salaat al-Istikhaarah* (The Prayer of Asking for Guidance on a Particular Matter)

Its wisdom: It is to submit to the command of Allah, to escape from one's supposed power and ability and to entrust the matter to Allah.

Its cause: *Salaat al-Istikhaarah* should be concerning those matters in which the person does not know where what is right lays. He is confused and goes back and forth between the two matters. However, if a matter's goodness is well-known, such as the acts of worship or doing good deeds, or if an act's evil is well-known, such as sinful acts or evil deeds, there is not to be any *salaat al-istikhaarah* to be performed over such matters. This is because there is no seeking of the best choice in a matter that is either sanctioned by the Shariah and prohibited by the Shariah. The mind of the one who makes this prayer must be free and should not already be intent on one particular course of action. If the proper circumstances occur, through the blessings of the prayer and supplication, what is best will become apparent to him. There is no harm if he repeats this prayer more than once.

Its description: The person should perform two *rakats* of prayer. In the first *rakah*, he reads *soorah al-Faatiha* and then, "O disbelievers" (*soorah* number 109). In the second *soorah*, he reads *soorah al-Faatiha* followed by, "Say: He is Allah, the One" (*soorah* number 112).[1]

After the salutations [to end the prayer,] the person raises his hands and supplicates,

---

[1] Until now, this translator could not find any justification for reading these particular chapters of the Quran in this prayer. Any two *rakat* voluntary prayer with any chapters being read seems to be sufficient. Allah knows best.—JZ

اللَّهُمَّ إِنِّي أَسْتَخِيرُكَ بِعِلْمِكَ وَأَسْتَقْدِرُكَ بِقُدْرَتِكَ وَأَسْأَلُكَ مِنْ فَضْلِكَ

الْعَظِيمِ فَإِنَّكَ تَقْدِرُ وَلَا أَقْدِرُ وَتَعْلَمُ وَلَا أَعْلَمُ وَأَنْتَ عَلَّامُ الْغُيُوبِ اللَّهُمَّ

إِنْ كُنْتَ تَعْلَمُ أَنَّ هَذَا الأَمْرَ خَيْرٌ لِي فِي دِينِي وَمَعَاشِي وَعَاقِبَةِ أَمْرِي

— أَوْ قَالَ فِي عَاجِلِ أَمْرِي وَآجِلِهِ — فَاقْدُرْهُ لِي وَإِنْ كُنْتَ تَعْلَمُ أَنَّ

هَذَا الْأَمْرَ شَرٌّ لِي فِي دِينِي وَمَعَاشِي وَعَاقِبَةِ أَمْرِي — أَوْ قَالَ فِي عَاجِلِ

أَمْرِي وَآجِلِهِ — فَاصْرِفْهُ عَنِّي وَاصْرِفْنِي عَنْهُ وَاقْدُرْ لِيَ الْخَيْرَ حَيْثُ

كَانَ ثُمَّ رَضِّنِي بِهِ

"O Allah, I seek Your guidance by Your knowledge; I seek the ability by Your ability; and I ask of Your great bounty. For verily, You have ability and I do not have ability. And You know and I do not know. You know the world of the Unseen. O Allah, if You know that this matter[1] is best for me in my religion, my living and the end of my affairs— or he says: best for my near future and best for my long-term future— then decree it for me. But if You know that it is worst for me in my religion, my living and the end of my affairs— or he says: worst for my near future and worst for my long-term future— then turn it away from me, turn me away from it and decree for me the good wherever it may be and then make me pleased with it.[2]" (Recorded by al-Bukhari.)

---

[1] At this point, the person mentions the affair that he is asking about.—JZ

[2] *Dhikr #52: Allaahumma ɛinnee ɛastakheeruka bi'ilmika wa ɛastaqdiruka bi-qudratika wa ɛas ɛaluka min fadlika-l-'aDHeemi fa ɛinnaka taqdiru wa laa ɛaqdiru wa ta'lamu wa laa ɛa'lamu wa ɛanta 'allaamu-l-guyoobi allaahumma ɛin kunta ta'lamu ɛanna hadha-l-ɛamra [and here the person mentions the affair] khairun lee fee deenee wa ma'aashee wa 'aaqibati ɛamree— or the person says, fee 'aajili ɛamree wa aajilihi—faqdurhu lee wa ɛin kunta ta'lamu ɛanna hadha-l-ɛamra sharrun lee fee deenee wa ma'aashee wa 'aaqibati ɛamree— or the person says, fee 'aajili ɛamree wa aajilihi— fasrifhu 'annee wasrifnee 'anhu waqdur liya-l-khaira haithu kaana thumma raddinee bih.*

(2) The Prostration Upon Reciting the Quran

If a person reads a verse concerning which there is a prostration, it is a preferred act for him to say the *takbeer*[1] ("*Allahu akbar*"), prostrate and say,

سَجَدَ وَجْهِي لِلَّذِي خَلَقَهُ وَشَقَّ سَمْعَهُ وَبَصَرَهُ بِحَوْلِهِ وَقُوَّتِهِ فَتَبَارَكَ اللهُ

أَحْسَنُ الْخَالِقِينَ

"I have prostrated my face to the One who created it and brought forth its hearing and seeing by His Power and Might. Blessed be Allah, the best of creators.[2]" (Recorded by al-Tirmidhi and al-Haakim.[3])

This is to be done whether one is currently in prayer or out of prayer. If it is done when one is not in prayer, it is not necessary for one to be in a state of purity.

(3) The Prostration of Thankfulness

It is recommended for one to prostrate out of thankfulness whenever he is granted a blessing or when a hardship is removed. This is based on the hadith that states, "Whenever anything happy or of good news came to the Prophet (peace be upon him), he would quickly prostrate in thanks to Allah." (Recorded by Abu Dawood.[4]) It is not necessary to make ablution for such a prostration.

---

1 There is a difference of opinion among the scholars as to whether it is necessary to say the *takbeer* before making the prostration of reading specific verses of the Quran.—JZ

2 *Dhikr* #53: *sajada wajhee lilladhee khalaqahu wa shaqqa sam'ahu wa basarahu bihaulihi wa quwwatihi fatabaaraka-llaahu ¢ahsanu-l-khaaliqeen.*

3 The complete wording is recorded by al-Haakim; al-Tirmidhi does not have the words, "Blessed be Allah…" According to al-Hilaali, this hadith is *sahih*. See al-Hilaali, vol. 1, p. 171.—JZ

4 According to al-Albani, this hadith is *sahih*. See al-Albani, *Sahih Sunan Abi Dawood*, vol. 2, p. 534.—JZ

(4) The Prayer of Repentance

The Messenger of Allah (peace be upon him) said,

مَا مِنْ رَجُلٍ يُذْنِبُ ذَنْبًا ثُمَّ يَقُومُ فَيَتَطَهَّرُ ثُمَّ يُصَلِّي ثُمَّ يَسْتَغْفِرُ اللَّهَ إِلاَّ
غَفَرَ اللَّهُ لَه

"No person commits a sin and then stands, purifies himself, prays and asks for Allah's forgiveness except that Allah forgives him." (Recorded by al-Tirmidhi.[1])
Allah says,

وَمَن يَعْمَلْ سُوٓءًا أَوْ يَظْلِمْ نَفْسَهُۥ ثُمَّ يَسْتَغْفِرِ ٱللَّهَ يَجِدِ ٱللَّهَ غَفُورًا
رَّحِيمًا

"And whoever does a wrong or wrongs himself and then seeks Allah's forgiveness will find Allah Forgiving and Merciful" (*al-Nisaa* 110).

(5) Upon Heading to the Mosque for the Morning (*Fajr*) Prayer

At such time, one says,

اللَّهُمَّ اجْعَلْ فِي قَلْبِي نُوراً وَفِي سَمْعِي نُوراً وَفِي بَصَرِي نُوراً وَعَنْ
يَمِينِي نُوراً وَعَنْ شِمَالِي نُوراً وَأَمَامِي نُوراً وَخَلْفِي نُوراً وَفَوْقِي نُوراً
وَتَحْتِي نُوراً وَاجْعَلْ لِي نُوراً

"O Allah, make a light in my heart; and in my hearing a light; and in my vision a light; and on my right a light; and

---

[1] In the hadith in al-Tirmidhi, the Prophet (peace be upon him) read *ali-Imraan* 135 after making the above statement. According to al-Albani, this hadith is *hasan*. See al-Albani, *Sahih Sunan al-Tirmidhi*, vol. 3, pp. 33-34.—JZ

on my left a light; and in front of me a light; and behind me a light; and above me a light; and below me a light; and make a light for me.[1]" (Recorded by Muslim.)

(6) During Hardship and Difficulties

During such times, one should say,

$$ لا إِلَهَ إِلاَّ اللَّهُ الْعَظِيمُ الْحَلِيمُ لا إِلَهَ إِلاَّ اللَّهُ رَبُّ الْعَرْشِ الْعَظِيمِ لا إِلَهَ إِلاَّ $$

$$ اللَّهُ رَبُّ السَّمَوَاتِ وَرَبُّ الأَرْضِ وَرَبُّ الْعَرْشِ الْكَرِيمِ $$

"There is none worthy of worship except Allah, the Great, the Forbearing. There is none worthy of worship except Allah, the Lord of the Great Throne. There is none worthy of worship except Allah, Lord of the heavens and Lord of the earth and Lord of the Noble Throne.[2]" [Recorded by al-Bukhari.] One also says,

$$ لا إِلَهَ إِلاَّ أَنْتَ سُبْحَانَكَ إِنِّي كُنْتُ مِنَ الظَّالِمِينَ $$

"There is none worthy of worship but You. Perfect are You. I was one of the wrongdoers.[3]" [Recorded by al-Tirmidhi.[4]] One also says,

$$ يَا حَيُّ يَا قَيُّومُ بِرَحْمَتِكَ أَسْتَغِيثُ $$

---

[1] *Dhikr* #54: *allaahumma-j'al fee qalbee nooran wa fee sam'ee nooran wa fee basaree nooran wa 'an yameenee nooran wa 'an shimaalee nooran wa samaamee nooran wa khalfee nooran wa fauqee nooran wa tahtee nooran wa-j'al lee nooran.*

[2] *Dhikr* #55: *laa silaaha illa-laahu-l-'aDHeemu-l-haleem. laa silaaha illa-laahu rabbu-l-'arshi-l-'aDHeem laa silaaha illa-laahu rabbu-samawaati wa rabbu-l-sardi wa rabbu-l-'arshi-l-kareem.*

[3] *Dhikr* #56: *laa silaaha silla santa subhaanaka sinnee kuntu mina-DHaalimeen.*

[4] This was the supplication that Jonah made when he was in the belly of the whale. According to al-Hilaali, this hadith is *sahih*. See al-Hilaali, vol. 1, p. 337.—JZ

"O Living One, O Sustainer, in Your mercy do I seek relief.[1]"
[Recorded by al-Tirmidhi.[2]]

(7) When the Person Faces a Distressing Matter, Worry or Concern

Under such circumstances, one should say,

اللَّهُمَّ إِنِّي عَبْدُكَ وَابْنُ عَبْدِكَ وَابْنُ أَمَتِكَ نَاصِيَتِي بِيَدِكَ مَاضٍ فِيَّ
حُكْمُكَ عَدْلٌ فِيَّ قَضَاؤُكَ أَسْأَلُكَ بِكُلِّ اسْمٍ هُوَ لَكَ سَمَّيْتَ بِهِ نَفْسَكَ
أَوْ عَلَّمْتَهُ أَحَدًا مِنْ خَلْقِكَ أَوْ أَنْزَلْتَهُ فِي كِتَابِكَ أَوِ اسْتَأْثَرْتَ بِهِ فِي عِلْمِ
الْغَيْبِ عِنْدَكَ أَنْ تَجْعَلَ الْقُرْآنَ رَبِيعَ قَلْبِي وَنُورَ صَدْرِي وَجَلَاءَ حُزْنِي
وَذَهَابَ هَمِّي

"O Allah, I am Your servant, the son of Your male servant and the son of Your female servant. My forelock is in Your hand. Your Judgment is continuously ruling over me, justly Your decree is over me. I ask of You, by every name You have, that You have named Yourself, or taught anyone of Your creation, or revealed in Your book or kept hidden in the unseen knowledge with You, to make the Quran the spring of my heart, a light of my breast, a departure for my sorrow

---

[1] *Dhikr* #57: *Yaa hayyu yaa qayyoomu birahmatika <u>a</u>astageet<u>h</u>.*
[2] Al-Hilaali concludes that this hadith is *hasan* due to supporting evidence. See al-Hilaali, vol. 1, p. 334.—JZ

and a release for my worry.[1]" (Recorded by Ahmad and al-Haakim.[2]) One also says,

يَا حَيُّ يَا قَيُّومُ بِرَحْمَتِكَ أَسْتَغِيثُ

"O Living One, O Sustainer, in Your mercy do I seek relief.[3]" (Recorded by al-Tirmidhi.[4])

(8) If one Fears a People

In this case, one should say,

اللَّهُمَّ إِنَّا نَجْعَلُكَ فِي نُحُورِهِمْ وَنَعُوذُ بِكَ مِنْ شُرُورِهِمْ

"O Allah, we place You on their necks and we seek refuge in You from their evil.[5]" (Recorded by Abu Dawood.[6])

(9) If a Matter Becomes Difficult or Hard for a Person

In such a case, one should say,

اللَّهُمَّ لاَ سَهْلَ إِلاَ مَا جَعَلْتَهُ سَهْلاً وَأَنْتَ تَجْعَلُ الْحَزْنَ إِذَا شِئْتَ سَهْلاً

---

[1] *Dhikr* #58: *allaahumma ғinnee 'abduka wa ibnu 'abdika ibnu ғamatika naasiyatee biyadik maadin fiya ḥukmuka 'adlun fiyya qada ғuka ғ as ғaluka bikulli-smin ḥuwa laka sammaita biḥi nafsaka ғau 'allamtaḥu ғaḥadan min kḥalqika ғau ғanzaltaḥu fee kitaabika ғawi-sta ғtḥarta biḥi fee 'ilma-l-gaibi 'indaka ғan taj'ala-l-qur ғaana rabee'a qalbee wa noora sadree wa jalaa ғa ḥuznee wa dḥaḥaaba ḥammee.*

[2] According to al-Albani, this hadith is *saḥih*. See Muhammad Nasir al-Deen al-Albani, *Silsilat al-Aḥadeeth al-Saheeḥa* (Damascus: al-Maktab al-Islaami, 1979), vol. 1, hadith #198.—JZ

[3] *Dhikr* #59: *Yaa ḥayyu yaa qayyoomu birahmatika ғastageetḥ.*

[4] Al-Hilaali concludes that this hadith is *ḥasan* due to supporting evidence. See al-Hilaali, vol. 1, p. 334.—JZ

[5] *Dhikr* #60: *Allaahumma ғinnaa naj'aluka fee nuboorihim wa na'oodḥu bika min sḥuroorihim.*

[6] According to al-Albani, this hadith is *saḥih*. See al-Albani, *Sabih al-Jaami*, vol. 2, p. 859.—JZ

"O Allah, there is nothing easy except what You make easy. You can make grief, if You wish, easy.[1]" (Recorded by ibn al-Sunee.[2])

(10) If Something Displeasing Happens to a Person

In such a case, the person should say,

قَدَّرَ اللهُ وَمَا شَاءَ فَعَلَ

"Allah has decreed and what He wills He does.[3]" "And avoid using the word, 'If,' for that opens the door for the acts of Satan." (Recorded by ibn al-Sunee.[4])

(11) When a Person is Overcome by a Matter

In this case, one says,

حَسْبُنَا اللَّهُ وَنِعْمَ الْوَكِيلُ

"Allah is sufficient for us and He is a great guardian.[5]" (Recorded by Abu Dawood.[6])

(12) If One is Tried by Debt

In such a case, one says,

اللَّهُمَّ اكْفِنِي بِحَلالِكَ عَنْ حَرَامِكَ وَأَغْنِنِي بِفَضْلِكَ عَمَّنْ سِوَاكَ

---

[1] *Dhikr* #61: *Allaahumma laa sahla ᶜilla maa ja'altahu sahlan wa ᶜanta taja'lu-l-hazna ᶜidha shi ᶜta sahlan.*

[2] According to al-Hilaali, this hadith is *sahih*. See al-Hilaali, vol. 1, p. 345.—JZ

[3] *Dhikr* #62: *qaddara-llaahu wa maa shaa ᶜa fa'ala.*

[4] According to al-Salafi, this hadith is *sahih*. See al-Salafi, p. 126.—JZ

[5] *Dhikr* #63: *hasbunaa-llaahu wa ni'ma-l-wakeel.*

[6] This hadith was recorded by Abu Dawood, Ahmad and ibn al-Sunee. According to al-Salafi, it is *hasan*. See al-Salafi, p. 126.—JZ

"O Allah, suffice me from Your lawful sources instead of what You have forbidden. And, by Your grace, make me not in need of anyone but You.[1]" (Recorded by al-Tirmidhi.[2])

(13) If One is Afflicted with a Hardship

Under such circumstances, one says,

مَا أَمَرَهُ اللَّهُ إِنَّا لِلَّهِ وَإِنَّا إِلَيْهِ رَاجِعُونَ اللَّهُمَّ أُجْرْنِي فِي مُصِيبَتِي وَأَخْلِفْ

لِي خَيْرًا مِنْهَا

"Whatever Allah has ordered! We belong to Allah and to Him we are returning. O Allah, reward me in my affliction and make what is after it better for me.[3]" (Recorded by Muslim.)

(14) If a Person Has Some Doubt about Faith Occurring to His Mind

In such a case, the person should seek refuge in Allah and put an end to those thoughts. Then he should say,

آمَنْتُ بِاللَّهِ وَرَسُولِهِ

"I believe in Allah and His messenger.[4]" (Recorded by al-Bukhari.[5])

---

[1] *Dhikr #64: Allaahumma-kfinee bihalaalika 'an haraamika wa eagninee bifadlika 'amman siwaak.*

[2] According to al-Hilaali, this hadith is *hasan*. See al-Hilaali, vol. 1, p. 348.—JZ

[3] *Dhikr #65: maa eamarahu-llaahu einnaa lilaahi wa einnaa eilaihi raaji'oona allaahumma-ejurnee fee museebatee wa eakhlif lee khairan minhaa.*

[4] *Dhikr #66: Aamantu bi-laahi wa rasoolihi.*

[5] Actually, only the first part is from al-Bukhari. Muslim has the words, "I believe in Allah." "I believe in Allah and His Messenger" is recorded by Ahmad.—JZ

(15) When One Feels the Disturbances of Satan while in Prayer, Reading the Quran and so forth

Under such circumstances, one should say,

أَعُوذُ بِاللهِ مِنَ الشَّيْطَانِ الرَّجِيْمِ

"I seek refuge in Allah from the accursed Satan.[1]" Then he should blow out on his left side three times. (Recorded by Muslim.)

(16) Words Said to Protect a Youngster

One should say,

أَعُوذُ بِكَلِمَاتِ اللّهِ التَّامَّةِ مِنْ كُلِّ شَيْطَانٍ وَهَامَّةٍ وَمِنْ كُلِّ عَيْنٍ لامَّةٍ

"I seek refuge in the perfect words of Allah from every devil, poisonous creature and from every harmful eye.[2]" (Recorded by al-Bukhari.)

(17) Upon Seeing Clouds about to Join Together

When one sees clouds about to join together, he should stop what he is doing, even if he is in prayer, and say,

اللَّهُمَّ إِنِّي أَعُوذُ بِكَ مِنْ شَرِّهَا

"O Allah, I seek refuge in You from its evil.[3]" (Recorded by Abu Dawood.[4])

---

[1] *Dhikr* #67: *ʿa'oodhu bi-laahi mina-shaitaanir-rajeem.*

[2] *Dhikr* #68: *ʿa'oodhu bikalimaati-laahi-ttaammati min kulli shaitaanin wa haammatin wa min kulli 'ainin laammah.*

[3] *Dhikr* #69: *allaahumma ʿinnee ʿa'oodhu bika min sharrihaa.*

[4] According to al-Albani, this hadith is *sahih*. See al-Albani, *Sahih Sunan Abi Dawood,* vol. 3, p. 960.—JZ

(18) Upon Hearing the Sound of Thunder

At such time, the following should be said,

اللَّهُمَّ لَا تَقْتُلْنَا بِغَضَبِكَ وَلَا تُهْلِكْنَا بِعَذَابِكَ وَعَافِنَا قَبْلَ ذَلِكَ

"O Allah, do not destroy us out of Your anger and do not destroy us by Your punishment. But forgive us before that." (Recorded by al-Tirmidhi.[1])

(19) What to Say when the Winds Become Strong

In this case, one says,

اللَّهُمَّ إِنِّي أَسْأَلُكَ خَيْرَهَا وَخَيْرَ مَا فِيهَا وَخَيْرَ مَا أُرْسِلَتْ بِهِ وَأَعُوذُ بِكَ

مِنْ شَرِّهَا وَشَرِّ مَا فِيهَا وَشَرِّ مَا أُرْسِلَتْ بِهِ

"O Allah, I ask you for the good of it and the good of what it contains and the good that it is sent with. And I seek refuge in You from its evil, the evil that it contains and the evil which with it has been sent.[2]" (Recorded by al-Bukhari.[3])

(20) When it Rains

When it rains, one should say,

اللَّهُمَّ صَيِّبًا نَافِعًا

"O Allah, [make it] a heavy beneficial rain.[4]" (Recorded by al-Bukhari.)

---

[1] According to al-Nawawi and al-Hilaali, this hadith is weak. See al-Hilaali, vol. 1, pp. 471-2.—JZ

[2] *Dhikr* #70: *Allaahumma innee as aluka khairahaa wa khaira maa feehaa wa khaira maa ursilat bihi wa a'oodhu bika min sharrihaa wa sharri maa feehaa wa sharri maa ursilat bihi.*

[3] It seems that this hadith is recorded only by Muslim and not by al-Bukhari. Allah knows best.—JZ

[4] *Dhikr* #71: *Allaahumma sayyiban naafi'an.*

(21)   When it Rains a Great Deal or One Fears that it will Become Harmful

In this case, one says,

اللَّهُمَّ حَوَالَيْنَا وَلا عَلَيْنَا اللَّهُمَّ عَلَى الآكَامِ وَالْجِبَالِ وَالآجَامِ وَالظِّرَابِ وَالأَوْدِيَةِ وَمَنَابِتِ الشَّجَرِ

"O Allah, around us and not upon us. O Allah, upon the plateaus, mountains, valleys, hills and roots of the trees.[1]" (Recorded by al-Bukhari.)

(22) After Rainfall

After rainfall, one says,

مُطِرْنَا بِفَضْلِ اللَّهِ وَرَحْمَتِهِ

"It rained upon us by the mercy and grace of Allah.[2]" (Recorded by al-Bukhari.)

(23) Upon Seeing the New Moon

When seeing the new moon, one says,

اللَّهُمَّ أَهْلِلْهُ عَلَيْنَا بِالْيُمْنِ وَالإِيمَانِ وَالسَّلامَةِ وَالإِسْلامِ رَبِّي وَرَبُّكَ اللَّهُ

"O Allah, bring the crescent over us with safety, faith, peace and Islam, my Lord and your Lord Allah.[3]" (Recorded by al-Tirmidhi.[4])

---

[1] *Dhikr* #72: *Allaahumma hawaalainaa wa laa 'alainaa allaahumma 'ala-l-aakaami wa-l-jibaali wa-l-aajaami wa-diraabi wa-l- ṣaudiyati wa manaabiti-shajar.*

[2] *Dhikr* #73: *mutirnaa bifadlilaahi wa rahmatihi.*

[3] *Dhikr* #74: *allahumma ṣahlilhu 'alainaa bi-l-yumni wa-l-ṣeemaani wa-salaamati wa-l-ṣislaami rabbee wa rabbuka-llaah.*

[4] According to al-Albani, this hadith is *sahih.* See al-Albani, *Sahih Sunan al-Tirmidhi,* vol. 3, p. 157.—JZ

(24) When One Sees the Moonrise

In this case, one says,

أَعُوذُ بِاللَّهِ مِنْ شَرِّ هَذَا الْغَاسِقِ إِذَا وَقَبَ

"I seek refuge in Allah from the evil of that darkness when it settles[1] [over the land].[2]" (Recorded by al-Tirmidhi.[3])

(25) When One Person Loves Another [For the Sake of Allah]

When one brother loves another, he should inform him of that by saying,

إِنِّي أُحِبُّكَ فِي اللَّهِ

"I love you for the sake of Allah.[4]" His brother's response should be,

أَحَبَّكَ الَّذِي أَحْبَبْتَنِي لَهُ

"May the One for whose sake you love me love you.[5]" (Recorded by Abu Dawood.[6])

(26) When a Person Sees His Brother Laughing

In this case, he should say to his brother,

أَضْحَكَ اللَّهُ سِنَّكَ

---

[1] *Waqab* means one that enters and leaves. The meaning of the hadith is that the Messenger of Allah (peace be upon him) ordered Aisha to make this supplication when the light of the moon disappears during the night or when the darkness becomes great.

[2] *Dhikr #75:* *a'oodhu bilaahi min sharri haadhaa-l-gaasiqi idhaa waqab.*

[3] According to al-Hilaali, this hadith is *sahih.* See al-Hilaali, vol. 1, p. 491.—JZ

[4] *Dhikr #76:* *innee uhibbuka fee-laah.*

[5] *Dhikr #77:* *ahabbaka-lladhee ahbabtanee lahu.*

[6] According to al-Albani, this hadith is *sahih.* See al-Albani, *Sahih Sunan Abi Dawood,* vol. 3, p. 965.—JZ

"May Allah keep you happy all your life.[1]" (Recorded by al-Bukhari.)

(27) Upon Sneezing

When one sneezes, he should put his clothing or hand over his mouth and restrain his sound. (Recorded by al-Tirmidhi.[2]) The sneezing person should say,

الْحَمْدُ لِلَّهِ

"All praise is due to Allah.[3]" His brother or companion should say to him,

يَرْحَمُكَ اللَّهُ

"May Allah have mercy on you.[4]" The one who sneezed should then say in reply to that,

يَهْدِيكُمُ اللَّهُ وَيُصْلِحُ بَالَكُمْ

"May Allah guide you and make your affairs better.[5]" (Recorded by al-Bukhari.) If a non-Muslim sneezes, the Muslim should say to him,

يَهْدِيكُمُ اللَّهُ وَيُصْلِحُ بَالَكُمْ

"May Allah guide you and make your affairs better.[6]" (Recorded by Abu Dawood.[7])

---

[1] *Dhikr* #78: *adhaka-llaahu sinnaka.*
[2] According to al-Albani, this hadith is *hasan sahih*. See al-Albani, *Sahih Sunan al-Tirmidhi*, vol. 2, p. 355.—JZ
[3] *Dhikr* #79: *al-hamdulilaah.*
[4] *Dhikr* #80: *yarhamuka-llaah.*
[5] *Dhikr* #81: *yahdeekumu-llaahu wa yuslihu baalakum.*
[6] *Dhikr* #82: *yahdeekumu-llaahu wa yuslihu baalakum.*
[7] According to al-Albani, this hadith is *sahih*. See al-Albani, *Sahih Sunan al-Tirmidhi*, vol. 2, p. 354.—JZ

(28) Upon Yawning

When yawning, one should restrain the yawn as much as possible. If he cannot stop the yawn, he should put his left hand over his mouth. (Recorded by Muslim.)

(29) Upon Hearing a Donkey Braying or a Dog Barking

Upon hearing such, one should say,

أَعُوْذُ بِاللهِ مِنَ الشَّيْطَانِ الرَّجِيْم

"I seek refuge in Allah from the accursed Satan.[1]" (Recorded by al-Bukhari and Abu Dawood.)

(30) Upon Hearing a Rooster Crow

When one hears a rooster crow, he should say,

أَسْأَلُ اللهَ مِنْ فَضْلِهِ

"I ask Allah from His bounty.[2]" (Recorded by al-Bukhari.)

(31) Before One Gets Up from a Gathering

In this case, one should say,

سُبْحَانَكَ اللّهُمَّ وَبِحَمْدِكَ أَشْهَدُ أَنْ لا إِلَهَ إِلاَّ أَنْتَ أَسْتَغْفِرُكَ وَأَتُوبُ إِلَيْكَ

"Perfect are You O Allah and to You is the Praise. I testify that there is none worthy of worship except You. I seek Your forgiveness and repent to You.[1]" (Recorded by al-Tirmidhi.[2])

---

[1] *Dhikr* #83: *a'oodhu bilaahi mina-shaitaani-rajeem.*
[2] *Dhikr* #84: *as alu-llaahu min fadlihi.*

(32) Upon Getting Angry

When a person gets angry, he should restrain his anger as much as possible and say,

أَعُوْذُ بِاللهِ مِنَ الشَّيْطَانِ الرَّجِيْمِ

"I seek refuge in Allah from the accursed Satan,[3]" and make ablution. (Recorded by al-Bukhari and Abu Dawood.[4])

(33) Upon Seeing One who is Being Afflicted

In such a case, one should say,

الْحَمْدُ لِلَّهِ الَّذِي عَافَانِي مِمَّا ابْتَلَاكَ بِهِ وَفَضَّلَنِي عَلَى كَثِيرٍ مِمَّنْ خَلَقَ تَفْضِيلًا

"All praise be to Allah who made me safe from what he afflicted you with and greatly blessed me above many of creation.[5]" (Recorded by al-Tirmidhi.[6])

---

[1] *Dhikr* #85: *subhaanaka-llaahumma wa bihamdika ashhadu an laa ilaaha illa anta astagfiruka wa atoobu ilaik.*

[2] According to al-Albani, this hadith is *sahih*. See al-Albani, *Sahih al-Jaami*, vol. 2, p. 1065. —JZ

[3] *Dhikr* #86: *a'oodhu bilaahi mina-shaitaani-rajeem.*

[4] The seeking of refuge from Satan is recorded by al-Bukhari. The making of ablution in order to lessen one's anger has been recorded by Abu Dawood and not al-Bukhari. Al-Albani and other modern day scholars have declared this hadith to be weak. Shuaib al-Arnaut, on the other hand, has declared its chain to be *hasan* and has said that those are mistaken when they call it weak. See Al-Albani, *Dhaeef al-Jaami*, p. 217; Al-Arnaut's footnotes to Abdul Rahmaan ibn Rajab, *Jaami al-Uloom wa al-Hikm* (Beirut: Muasassah al-Risaalah, 1991), vol. 1, p. 366.—JZ

[5] *Dhikr* #87: *al-hamdulilaahi-lladhee 'aafaanee mimmaa-btalaaka bihi wa fadalanee 'alaa katheerin mimman khalaqa tafdeelan.*

[6] According to al-Albani, this hadith is *hasan*. See al-Albani, *Sahih al-Jaami*, vol. 2, pp. 1072-1073.—JZ

(34) Upon Entering the Marketplace

In this case, one should say,

لا إِلَهَ إِلاَّ اللَّهُ وَحْدَهُ لا شَرِيكَ لَهُ لَهُ الْمُلْكُ وَلَهُ الْحَمْدُ يُحْيِي وَيُمِيتُ
وَهُوَ حَيٌّ لا يَمُوتُ بِيَدِهِ الْخَيْرُ وَهُوَ عَلَى كُلِّ شَيْءٍ قَدِيرٌ

"There is none worthy of worship except Allah, alone, without
any partner with Him. For Him is the Dominion and to Him is
the praise. He gives life and He brings about death; He is
living and does not die. In His hand is all good and He has
power over all things.[1]" (Recorded by al-Tirmidhi.[2])

(35) When Someone Does a Good Deed For Another

If a person does some good towards another, the
latter should do a similar good act in return. If he is not able
to, he should pray for the person and say,

جَزَاكَ اللهُ خَيْراً

"May Allah reward you well.[3]" In that case, one has gone far
enough in thanking him. (Recorded by Abu Dawood and al-
Tirmidhi.[4])

---

[1] *Dhikr* #88: *laa ¢ilaaha ¢illa-llaahu wahdahu laa shareeka lahu lahu-l-
mulku wa lahu-l-hamdu yuhyee wa yumeetu wa huwa hayyun laa yamootu
biyadihi-l-khairu wa huwa 'ala kulli shai¢in qadeer.*

[2] According to al-Albani, this hadith is *hasan*. See al-Albani, *Sahih al-Jaami*, vol. 2,
p. 1070.—JZ

[3] *Dhikr* #89: *jazaaku-llaahu khairan.*

[4] According to al-Albani, this hadith is *sahih*. See al-Albani, *Sahih al-Jaami*, vol. 2,
p. 1089.—JZ

(36) Upon Repaying a Debt

If a person borrows money from another and repays him, he should pray for him by saying, as is stated in a hadith,

بَارَكَ اللَّهُ لَكَ فِي أَهْلِكَ وَمَالِكَ إِنَّمَا جَزَاءُ السَّلَفِ الْحَمْدُ وَالأَدَاءُ

"May Allah bless you in your family and wealth. Certainly, the reward for a loan is thanks and repayment.[1]" (Recorded by ibn al-Sunee.[2])

(37) Upon Seeing the First Fruits of Harvest

At that time, one should say,

اللَّهُمَّ بَارِكْ لَنَا فِي ثَمَرِنَا وَبَارِكْ لَنَا فِي مَدِينِتِنَا وَبَارِكْ لَنَا فِي صَاعِنَا

وَبَارِكْ لَنَا فِي مُدِّنَا

"O Allah, bless us in our fruits, bless us in our city, bless us in our sa's and bless us in our mudds.[3]"[4] Then the person should give some of it to the youngest child present. (Recorded by Muslim.)

(38) Upon Seeing Something Wonderful or Amazing

In this case, one should say,

مَا شَاءَ اللَّهُ لا قُوَّةَ إِلاَّ بِاللَّهِ

---

[1] *Dhikr* #90: *baaraka-llaahu laka fee ꜱahlika wa maalika ꜱinnamaa jazaa ꜱu-salafi-l-ḥamdu wa-l-ꜱadaa.*

[2] Actually, this hadith is also recorded by Ahmad, al-Nasaai and ibn Majah. Al-Albani declared it *sahih* while al-Hilaali said that it is *"hasan* Allah willing." See al-Albani, *Sahih al-Jaami*, vol. 1, p. 464; al-Hilaali, vol. 2, p. 765.—JZ

[3] *Dhikr* #91: *Allaahumma baarik lanaa fee thamarinaa wa baarik lanaa fee madeenatinaa wa baarik lanaa fee saa'inaa wa baarik lanaa fee muddanaa.*

[4] *Sa'* and *mudd* are two types of measures; a *mudd* is the amount that two hands cupped together holds and a *sa'* is four *mudd*.

"Whatever Allah wills. There is no power except in Allah,[1]"
as Allah says in *soorah al-Kahf,*

$$وَلَوْلَا إِذْ دَخَلْتَ جَنَّتَكَ قُلْتَ مَا شَاءَ ٱللَّهُ لَا قُوَّةَ إِلَّا بِٱللَّهِ$$

"Why did you not say upon entering your garden, 'Whatever
Allah wills. There is no power except in Allah'" (*al-Kahf* 39).
One should also say,

$$اللهُمَّ بَارِكْ فِيهِ$$

"O Allah, bless it.[2]" This is based on the hadith which states,

$$إِذَا رَأَى أَحَدُكُمْ مِنْ أَخِيهِ أَوْ مِنْ نَفْسِهِ أَوْ مِنْ مَالِهِ مَا يُعْجِبُهُ فَلْيُبَرِّكْهُ$$

$$فَإِنَّ الْعَيْنَ حَقٌّ$$

"If one of you sees something from his brother or from himself
or from his wealth that amazes him, he should seek blessings
for it as the evil eye is a reality." (Recorded by Ahmad and
al-Haakim.[3])

(39) When One Sees Something that He Loves

In this case, one should say,

$$الْحَمْدُ لِلَّهِ الَّذِي بِنِعْمَتِهِ تَتَمُّ الصَّالِحَاتِ$$

"All praise be to Allah, the One by Whose blessings the
righteous deeds are completed.[4]" (Recorded by al-Haakim.[5])

---

[1] *Dhikr* #92: *maa shaa sallaahu laa quwwata silla bi-laah.*

[2] *Dhikr* #93: *allaahumma baarik feeh.*

[3] According to al-Albani, this hadith is *sahih.* See al-Albani, *Sahih al-Jaami*, vol. 1, p. 158.—JZ

[4] *Dhikr* #94: *al-hamdulilaahi-ladhee bini'matihi tatammu-saalihaat.*

[5] According to al-Hilaali, this hadith is *hasan* due to its supporting evidence. See al-Hilaali, vol. 2, pp. 783-784.—JZ

(40) When One Sees Something Disliked

In this case, one says,

$$\text{الْحَمْدُ لِلَّهِ عَلَى كُلِّ حَالٍ}$$

"Praise be to Allah under all circumstances.[1]" (Recorded by al-Haakim.[2])

(41) Upon Purchasing a Riding Animal, Vehicle and So Forth

On such an occasion, one says,

$$\text{اللَّهُمَّ إِنِّي أَسْأَلُكَ خَيْرَهَا وَخَيْرَ مَا جَبَلْتَهَا عَلَيْهِ وَأَعُوذُ بِكَ مِنْ شَرِّهَا}$$

$$\text{وَمِنْ شَرِّ مَا جَبَلْتَهَا عَلَيْهِ}$$

"O Allah, I ask of You for its good and the good of what You have made it incline towards. And I seek refuge in You from its evil and the evil You have made it incline to.[3]" (Recorded by Abu Dawood.[4])

(42) During Times of Difficulty, Grief or Worry

(a) In the *Sahih*s of al-Bukhari and Muslim it is recorded on the authority of ibn Abbas that the Messenger of Allah (peace be upon him) used to say the following during times of difficulty,

---

[1] *Dhikr #95: al-hamdu-lilaahi 'alaa kulli haal.*

[2] According to al-Hilaali, this hadith is *hasan* due to its supporting evidence. See al-Hilaali, vol. 2, pp. 783-784.—JZ

[3] *Dhikr #96: Allaahumma ɛinnee ɛasɛaluka khairahaa wa khaira maa jabaltahaa 'alaihi wa ɛa'oodhu bika min sharrihaa wa min sharri maa jabaltahaa 'alaih.*

[4] According to al-Hilaali, this hadith is *hasan*. See al-Hilaali, vol. 2, p. 700.—JZ

لَا إِلَهَ إِلَّا اللَّهُ الْعَظِيمُ الْحَلِيمُ لَا إِلَهَ إِلَّا اللَّهُ رَبُّ الْعَرْشِ الْعَظِيمِ لَا إِلَهَ إِلَّا
اللَّهُ رَبُّ السَّمَوَاتِ وَرَبُّ الْأَرْضِ وَرَبُّ الْعَرْشِ الْكَرِيمِ

"There is none worthy of worship except Allah, the Great, the Forbearing. There is none worthy of worship except Allah, the Lord of the Great Throne. There is none worthy of worship except Allah, Lord of the heavens and Lord of the earth and Lord of the Noble Throne.[1]"

(b) Anas (may Allah be pleased with him) reported that the Prophet (peace be upon him) would say, when a matter was bothering him,

يَا حَيُّ يَا قَيُّومُ بِرَحْمَتِكَ أَسْتَغِيثُ

"O Living One, O Sustainer, in Your mercy do I seek relief.[2]" (Recorded by al-Tirmidhi and others.[3])

(c) Abu Bakrah reported that the Prophet (peace be upon him) had said,

دَعَوَاتُ الْمَكْرُوبِ > اللَّهُمَّ رَحْمَتَكَ أَرْجُو فَلَا تَكِلْنِي إِلَى نَفْسِي طَرْفَةَ
عَيْنٍ أَصْلِحْ لِي شَأْنِي كُلَّهُ لَا إِلَهَ إِلَّا أَنْتَ <

"The supplications of the one in distress is: O Allah, I hope for Your mercy. Do not put me in my own charge for even the blinking of an eye. And make all of my affairs better and good. There is none worthy of worship except You.[4]" (Recorded by Ahmad and Abu Dawood.[5])

---

[1] *Dhikr* #97: *laa ṣilaaha illa-laahu-l-'adeemu-l-ḥaleem. laa ṣilaaha illa-laahu rabbu-l-'arshi-l-'adeemi laa ṣilaaha illa-laahu rabbu-samawaati wa rabbu-l-ṣardi wa rabbu-l-'arshi-l-kareem.*

[2] *Dhikr* #98: *Yaa ḥayyu yaa qayyoomu biraḥmatika ṣastageeth.*

[3] Al-Hilaali concludes that this hadith is *basan* due to supporting evidence. See al-Hilaali, vol. 1, p. 334.—JZ

[4] *Dhikr* #99: *Allaahumma raḥmataka ṣarjoo falaa takilnee ṣilaa nafsee tarfata 'ainin ṣaslib lee sha ṣnee kullabu laa ṣilaaha ṣilla ṣanta.*

[5] According to al-Albani, this hadith is *basan.* See al-Albani, *Sabib al-Jaami*, vol. 1, p. 638.—JZ

(d) Asmaa bint Umais narrated that the Messenger of Allah (peace be upon him) said, "Shall I not teach you words that you may say during times of distress? They are,

اللهُ اللَّهُ رَبِّي لا أُشْرِكُ بِهِ شَيْئًا

'Allah is my Lord. I do not associate anything with Him.'[1]" (Recorded by Ahmad, Abu Dawood and others.[2])

(e) In *Sahih Muslim* it is recorded from Umm Salama that she heard the Messenger of Allah (peace be upon him) say, "No servant is inflicted with an infliction but if he says,

إِنَّا لِلَّهِ وَإِنَّا إِلَيْهِ رَاجِعُونَ اللَّهُمَّ أُجُرْنِي فِي مُصِيبَتِي وَأَخْلِفْ لِي خَيْرًا مِنْهَا

'We belong to Allah and to Him we are returning. O Allah, reward me in my affliction and make what is after it better for me,[3]' Allah will reward him for his affliction and will give him a better replacement." Umm Salama stated that she said those words as the Prophet (peace be upon him) had told her when her husband Abu Salama died and, she said, "Allah gave me some one better than him as a replacement: the Messenger of Allah (peace be upon him)."

(f) Al-Bukhari recorded from ibn Abbas that when Abraham was put into the fire, he said the words,

حَسْبُنَا اللَّهُ وَنِعْمَ الْوَكِيلُ

"Allah is sufficient for us and [He is] the best Disposer of affairs.[4]" The Prophet Muhammad (peace be upon him) also said that when the people were telling him, "The people have gathered against you, so fear them." That increased their faith and they said, " Allah is sufficient for us and [He is] the best Disposer of affairs."

---

[1] *Dhikr* #100: *Allaah Allaahu rabbee laa ṣushriku bihi shaiṣan.*

[2] According to al-Hilaali, this hadith is *sahih*. See al-Hilaali, vol. 1, p. 336.—JZ

[3] *Dhikr* #101: *ṣinnaa lilaahi wa ṣinna ṣilaihi raaji'oona allaahumma-ṣjurnee fee museebatee wa ṣakhlif lee khairan minhaa.*

[4] *Dhikr* #102: *hasbunaa-llaahu wa ni'ma-l-wakeel.*

Al-Bukhari also recorded from ibn Abbaas that the last statement that Abraham made when he was cast into the fire was, "Allah is sufficient for us and [He is] the best Disposer of affairs."

(16) Words of Remembrance Related to the Ill and Visiting the Sick

(1) The most beneficial incantation and the one with the greatest effect is the one that is done by the person himself. This is what is shown in the text. It is the opposite of the popular practice of people today who go out seeking someone to read the Quran, even if he is an ignorant person or a commoner.

(2) Reciting *soorah al-Faatiha* is the most important and most beneficial of what one can read over the ill. This is due to what this great chapter contains of purity in the worship of Allah, praise for Him, entrusting all of one's affairs to Him, seeking relief from Him, putting one's trust in Him, and asking Him for all the collective good. Furthermore, it is recorded as an incantation in the texts, such as what is in *Sahih al-Bukhari* concerning the scorpion bite.

(3) When one visits an ill person, he should say,

لَا بَأْسَ طَهُورٌ إِنْ شَاءَ اللَّهُ

"No harm, purification, Allah willing.[1]" He should use his right hand to wipe over the ill person and also say,

اللَّهُمَّ رَبَّ النَّاسِ أَذْهِبِ الْبَاسَ اشْفِهِ وَأَنْتَ الشَّافِي لَا شِفَاءَ إِلاَّ شِفَاؤُكَ شِفَاءً لَا يُغَادِرُ سَقَمًا

"O Allah, the Lord of Mankind, remove the hardship. Cure him as You are the Curer. There is no cure except for Your

---

[1] *Dhikr* #103: *laa ba ssa tahoorun sin shaa sa-llaah.*

cure, a cure that leaves behind no sickness.[1]" (Recorded by al-Bukhari.)

  (4) When saying an incantation for the ill person, one should say,

بِاسْمِ اللَّهِ أَرْقِيكَ مِنْ كُلِّ شَيْءٍ يُؤْذِيكَ مِنْ شَرِّ كُلِّ نَفْسٍ أَوْ عَيْنٍ

حَاسِدٍ اللَّهُ يَشْفِيكَ بِاسْمِ اللَّهِ أَرْقِيكَ

"In the name of Allah do I make this incantation over you from everything that harms you, from the harm of every soul or envious evil eye. May Allah cure you. In the name of Allah I make this incantation over you.[2]" (Recorded by Muslim.)

  (5) If a person complains about a pain in a part of his body, he should put his hand over the part which is hurting and say,

بِسْمِ اللهِ

"In the name of Allah,[3]" three times. He should also say the following seven times,

أَعُوذُ بِاللَّهِ وَقُدْرَتِهِ مِنْ شَرِّ مَا أَجِدُ وَأُحَاذِرُ

"I seek refuge in Allah and His Power from the evil that I experience and what I fear.[4]" (Recorded by Muslim.)

  (6) Incantation from the Evil Eye:

  (6a) The Messenger of Allah (peace be upon him) said,

الْعَيْنُ حَقٌّ وَلَوْ كَانَ شَيْءٌ سَابَقَ الْقَدَرَ سَبَقَتْهُ الْعَيْنُ

"The Evil Eye is a reality. If there were anything that could precede pre-destination, the Evil Eye would precede it." (Recorded by Muslim.)

---

[1] *Dhikr* #104: *allaahumma rabba-naasi ɛadhhibi-baasa ishfihi wa ɛanta-shaafee laa shifaaɛa ɛillaa shifaaɛuka shifaaɛan laa yugaadiru saqaman.*

[2] *Dhikr* #105: *bismilaahi ɛarqeeka min kulli shai ɛin yu ɛdheeka min sharri kulli nafsin ɛau 'aini haasidin allaahu yashfeeka bismilaahi ɛarqeek.*

[3] *Dhikr* #106: *bismilaah.*

[4] *Dhikr* #107: *ɛa'oodhu bi-laahi wa qudratihi min sharri maa ɛajidu wa ɛuhaadhir.*

(6b) Aisha said, "The Messenger of Allah (peace be upon him) ordered me or ordered the use of incantation from the Evil Eye." (Recorded by al-Bukhari.)

(6c) Being afflicted by the Evil Eye could be from humans or from jinn. It is mentioned in *Sahih al-Bukhari* that the Prophet (peace be upon him) saw in Umm Salama's house a young girl who had a darkness in her face. The Prophet (peace be upon him) then said,

استرقوا لها فإن بها النظرة

"Seek an incantation for her, for she is under the effect of an Evil Eye." (Recorded by al-Bukhari.)

(6d) The one who inflicted the evil eye should be ordered to do what the Prophet (peace be upon him) ordered Aamir ibn Rabeeah to do. Aamir ibn Rabeeah saw Sahl ibn Hunaif making *ghusl*. Aamir exclaimed, "By Allah, I have never seen what I saw today, not even among those young women who have not gone out of their houses." [He was commenting on the whiteness of Sahl's skin.] Immediately, Sahl fell to the ground ill. Aamir was brought to the Prophet (peace be upon him). The Prophet (peace be upon him) was furious with him and told him, "Why does one of you try to kill his brother. Why didn't you invoke blessings for him. You should wash yourself for him." So Aamir washed himself for Sahl by washing his face, hands, forearms, knees and ends of his feet and washed his under clothing in a bowl of water. Then he poured that water over Sahl and he became fine and went off with the people. (Recorded by Maalik in *al-Muwatta*.[1])

(6e) Among those aspects that will protect a Muslim from the evil of the Evil Eye as well as all evil is the continual usage of the words of remembrance and supplications during the morning and evening. Furthermore, a Muslim should not be greatly concerned with the Evil Eye. Instead, a Muslim should put his trust in Allah and, to the best of his ability, he should not expect such evil to occur. Not openly displaying

---

[1] This hadith was also recorded by ibn Maajah. According to al-Albani, it is *sahih*. See al-Albani, *Sahih Sunan ibn Majah*, vol. 2, p. 265.—JZ

good qualities as well as refraining one's tongue from describing such qualities in an exaggerated and over done way will also protect one from the Evil Eye.

(7) The cure for the one who is bewitched:

The thing which is most beneficial in protecting one from magic and all evil is the continual use of the words of remembrance in the morning and late afternoon, the reciting of "the Verse of the Throne" (*al-Baqara* 255), the reciting of *soorah al-Ikhlaas* (*soorah* number 112) and the reciting of the last two *soorahs* of the Quran, those that encompass seeking refuge in Allah. These should be read after every prayer and at the time of going to sleep. One should also read the last two verses of *soorah al-Baqara* every night. The one who is kept from having sexual intercourse with his wife due to magic should[1] take seven leaves of the green *sadar* plant, or something similar to that, and should pulverize them with a stone and put them in a bowl, pour enough water that one needs to make *ghusl* over them and recite over them "the Verse of the Throne," *soorah al-Kaafiroon* (*soorah* number 109), *soorah al-Ikhlaas* (*soorah* number 112), *soorah al-Falaq* (*soorah* number 113), *soorah al-Naas* (*soorah* number 114), and the verses of *soorah al-Araaf* concerning magic—which are,

﴿ وَأَوْحَيْنَآ إِلَىٰ مُوسَىٰٓ أَنْ أَلْقِ عَصَاكَ فَإِذَا هِـىَ تَلْقَفُ مَا يَأْفِكُونَ ۝ فَوَقَعَ ٱلْحَقُّ وَبَطَلَ مَا كَانُوا يَعْمَلُونَ ۝ فَغُلِبُوا هُنَالِكَ وَٱنقَلَبُوا صَٰغِرِينَ ۝ ﴾

"And We inspired to Moses, 'Throw your staff,' and at once it devoured what they were falsifying. So the truth was established, and abolished was what they used to do. And they [Pharaoh and his people] were overcome right there and

---

[1] The following is taken from Abdul Azeez ibn Baaz, *Majmooat Fatawa wa Maqaalaat Mutanawaab*, vol. 3.

became debased" (*al-Araaf* 117-119). One should also recite the relevant verses from *soorah Yoonus*— which are,

وَقَالَ فِرْعَوْنُ ٱئْتُونِى بِكُلِّ سَٰحِرٍ عَلِيمٍ ۝ فَلَمَّا جَآءَ ٱلسَّحَرَةُ قَالَ لَهُم مُّوسَىٰٓ أَلْقُوا۟ مَآ أَنتُم مُّلْقُونَ ۝ فَلَمَّآ أَلْقَوْا۟ قَالَ مُوسَىٰ مَا جِئْتُم بِهِ ٱلسِّحْرُ إِنَّ ٱللَّهَ سَيُبْطِلُهُۥٓ إِنَّ ٱللَّهَ لَا يُصْلِحُ عَمَلَ ٱلْمُفْسِدِينَ ۝ وَيُحِقُّ ٱللَّهُ ٱلْحَقَّ بِكَلِمَٰتِهِۦ وَلَوْ كَرِهَ ٱلْمُجْرِمُونَ

"And Pharaoh said, 'Bring to me ever learned magician.' So when the magicians came, Moses said to them, 'Cast whatever you will cast.' And when they did cast [their magic], Moses said, 'What you have brought is only magic. Indeed, Allah will expose its worthlessness. Certainly, Allah does not make good the works of evildoers. And Allah will establish the truth by His words, even if the criminals dislike it'" (*Yoonus* 79-82). One should also recite the following from *soorah Taha*,

قَالُوا۟ يَٰمُوسَىٰٓ إِمَّآ أَن تُلْقِىَ وَإِمَّآ أَن نَّكُونَ أَوَّلَ مَنْ أَلْقَىٰ ۝ قَالَ بَلْ أَلْقُوا۟ فَإِذَا حِبَالُهُمْ وَعِصِيُّهُمْ يُخَيَّلُ إِلَيْهِ مِن سِحْرِهِمْ أَنَّهَا تَسْعَىٰ ۝ فَأَوْجَسَ فِى نَفْسِهِۦ خِيفَةً مُّوسَىٰ ۝ قُلْنَا لَا تَخَفْ إِنَّكَ أَنتَ ٱلْأَعْلَىٰ ۝ وَأَلْقِ مَا فِى يَمِينِكَ تَلْقَفْ مَا صَنَعُوٓا۟ إِنَّمَا صَنَعُوا۟ كَيْدُ سَٰحِرٍ وَلَا يُفْلِحُ ٱلسَّاحِرُ حَيْثُ أَتَىٰ

"They said, 'O Moses, either you cast or we will be the first to cast.' He said, 'Rather, you cast.' And suddenly their ropes and staffs seemed to him that they were moving [like snakes]. And Moses sensed within himself apprehension. We [Allah] said, 'Fear not. Indeed, you will be superior. And throw what is in your right hand; it will swallow up what they have crafted. What they have crafted is only the trick of a magician, and the magician will never succeed wherever he may be'" (Taha 65-69).

After reading all of that over the water, the person should drink from it three times and then wash himself with the remainder of the water. That should bring an end to his affliction, Allah willing. If he needs to do that twice or more often, there is no harm in doing it until the disease is removed.[1]

Another way of curing the effect of magic, and this is one of the most beneficial means, is to do one's best to find the place in the earth, mountain or elsewhere in which the instruments used by the magician are present. If this is known, taken out and destroyed, the effect of the magic will come to an end. These are some of the clear matters that are easy for me to present concerning how to protect oneself from magic

---

[1] As the author mentioned, the above concerning the reading of specific verses over ground leaves in water and so forth is taken from Abdul Azeez ibn Baaz, *Majmoo Fatawa wa Maqaalaat Mutanwaah* (Riyadh: Maktabah al-Maarif, 1992), vol. 3, pp. 279-280. Virtually the same practice has also been mentioned in the following works related to magic: Waheed Baali, *al-Saarim al-Bataar fi al-Tasaddee lil-Saharati-l-Ashraar* (Jeddah: Maktaba al-Sahaaba, 1992), pp. 195-196; Misfur al-Damaini, *Al-Sihr: Haqeeqatuhu wa Hikmuhu...* (1991), pp. 63-64 (quoting verbatim ibn Baaz); Hayaat Akhdar, *Mauqif al-Islaam min al-Sihr* (Jeddah: Dar al-Mujtama, 1995), vol. 2, pp. 597-8 (see also pp. 620-621). The following work simply mentions the verses mentioned above as being effective against magic: Umar al-Ashqar, *Aalim al-Sihr wa al-Shaoowadhah* (Kuwait: Maktabah al-Falaah, 1989), p. 212. However, none of these works present any strong evidence for such a practice, especially the aspect of grinding leaves, putting them in water and reading over them. It is very possible that what is effective is simply the reading of those particular verses or other verses without any need to read them over water, drink them and bathe in them. For something of this nature, some sort of evidence or narration should be given by the scholar. Again, none of the authors who mentioned such a practice offered any evidence whatsoever. Allah knows best.—JZ

and cure its effect. And Allah is the source of grace and guidance.[1]

 (8) It is not allowed to wish for death due to some harm that has come to a person. If a person insists upon such an act, he should say,

اللّٰهُمَّ أَحْيِنِي مَا كَانَتِ الْحَيَاةُ خَيْرًا لِي وَتَوَفَّنِي إِذَا كَانَتِ الْوَفَاةُ خَيْرًا

لِي

"O Allah, give me life as long as life is best for me and give me death if death is best for me.[2]" (Recorded by al-Bukhari.)

 (9) It is recommended to encourage the one on his deathbed to say, "There is none worthy of worship except Allah." This is based on the following hadith,

لَقِّنُوا مَوْتَاكُمْ > لا إِلَهَ إِلاَّ اللّٰهُ <

"Instruct those among you who are about to die to say, 'There is none worthy of worship except Allah.'" (Recorded by Muslim.) One should not insist upon the ill person to repeat this often in order not to irritate him.

 (10) What to say when one is with an ill person or deceased: the Messenger of Allah (peace be upon him) said,

إِذَا حَضَرْتُمُ الْمَرِيضَ أَوِ الْمَيِّتَ فَقُولُوا خَيْرًا فَإِنَّ الْمَلَائِكَةَ يُؤَمِّنُونَ عَلَى

مَا تَقُولُونَ

"If you are in the presence of the ill or deceased, then only say what is good for the angels say, 'Amen,' to what you say." (Recorded by Muslim.)

 (11) When one hears about the death of his companion, he should say,

---

[1] This ends the portion quoted from Abdul Azeez ibn Baaz.—JZ

[2] *Dhikr #108: allaahumma ẹahyinee maa kaanati-l-ḥayaatu khairan lee wa tawaffanee ẹidhaa kaanati-l-wafaatu khairan lee.*

إِنَّا لِلَّهِ وَإِنَّا إِلَيْهِ رَاجِعُوْنَ وَإِنَّا إِلَى رَبِّنَا لَمُنْقَلِبُوْنَ اللَّهُمَّ اكْتُبْهُ عِنْدَكَ فِيْ

الْمُحْسِنِيْنَ وَاجْعَلْ كِتَابَهُ فِيْ عِلِّيِّيْنَ وَاخْلُفْهُ فِيْ أَهْلِهِ فِيْ الْغَابِرِيْنَ وَلَا

تَحْرِمْنَا أَجْرَهُ وَلاَ تَفْتِنَّا بَعْدَهُ

"We belong to Allah and unto Him we are returning. It is towards our Lord that we are journeying. O Allah, record him with You among the doers of excellence and place his book in the *Illiyeen*.[1] Leave someone who will take his place among those left behind. Do not prevent us from his reward and do not put us to trial after him." (Recorded by ibn al-Sunee.[2])

(12) What softens or removes the hardship of an infliction[3]:

A Muslim may be tried or face hardships with respect to his own self, family or wealth. The stronger a person's faith in Allah is, the more he will restrain himself, be patient and expect rewards from Allah for that hardship. His reward from Allah will be to the extent of his patience and his acting in hope for reward.

The following are some of the aspects that may soften or lessen the pain of a hardship or difficulty:

a) Patience: Allah has said in the Quran,

وَبَشِّرِ الصَّـٰبِرِينَ ۝ الَّـذِينَ إِذَآ أَصَـٰبَتْهُم مُّصِيبَةٌ قَالُوٓاْ إِنَّا لِلَّهِ وَإِنَّآ إِلَيْهِ رَٰجِعُونَ ۝ أُوْلَـٰٓئِكَ عَلَيْهِمْ صَلَوَٰتٌ مِّن رَّبِّهِمْ وَرَحْمَةٌ وَأُوْلَـٰٓئِكَ هُمُ الْمُهْتَدُونَ

---

[1] This is what is mentioned in *soorah al-Mutaffifeen*, verse 18. It is the record of the righteous.—JZ

[2] This hadith has been declared weak by al-Salafi and al-Hilaali. See al-Salafi, p. 198; al-Hilaali, vol. 1, p. 391.—JZ

[3] See ibn al-Qayyim, *Zaad al-Maad fi Huda Khair al-Ibaad*, vol. 4.

"Give glad tidings to those who are patient, who, when disaster strikes them, say, 'Indeed, we belong to Allah, and indeed to Him we will return.' Those are the ones upon whom are blessings from their Lord and mercy. And it is those who are the [rightly] guided" (*al-Baqara* 155-157).

b) The person should remind himself that he himself, his family and his wealth belong, in reality, to Allah. In reality, the slave is only borrowing these from Allah. When Allah takes it back, it is like the owner taking back his property from the one who borrowed it from him.

c) The person should also recall that the journey of the servant is to depart from this world and he is returning to Allah, his lord and guardian in truth.

d) The person must also believe in certainty that what afflicted him was not going to miss him and what misses him was not going to afflict him.

e) The person should consider the affliction he is suffering and realize that His Lord has left him something similar to what he has lost or better than it or has stored for him, if he is patient and pleased with Allah's decree, something that is far greater and superior to anything that he has lost. He should also realize that if Allah had willed to make his affliction much worse, He could have done so.

f) The person can put out the fire of his affliction by looking to the example of all the people around him who suffer afflictions. He will then realize that everyone is facing the same kind of difficulties. If he looks to his right, he will see that people are facing trials. If he glances to his left, he will find people in disasters and loss. If he searched the entire world, he will find that everyone is facing a trial: either someone has lost a loved one or is facing something disliked to him. Happiness in this world is really only a dream or like a passing cloud. If a person laughs a little, he will cry a great deal. If he is happy for a day, he will be unhappy for a long period of time. If a person enjoys himself a little, he will find a long period when he is prevented from such pleasures. No place is filled with goodness except that it is also filled with lessons that one must learn from. No day of happiness comes to a person except that hidden for him will be a day of harm.

g) The person should realize that being impatient and worried does not repel the affliction. Indeed, it makes it worse. In reality, it is a type of increase in the disease.

h) The person should also realize the reward for patience, submission and recognizing that we all belong to Allah and are returning to him is greater than the affliction itself.

i) The person should also realize that being impatient simply makes his enemy rejoice, harms his friend, displeases his Lord, pleases his devil, wipes away his reward and weakens his soul. If the person is patient and expects his reward from Allah, his devil will be defeated and rebuked in despair. Furthermore, his Lord will be pleased with him, his friend will be happy, his enemy will be unhappy. He will relieve his brethren of their worry and burden. Indeed, he will offer them condolences before they offer him condolences. That is the constancy and great completion. That is what should be done and not the striking of the cheek, tearing of the clothes, screams of pain and anguish and anger with what has been decreed.

j) The person should also realize that the bitter aspects of this world are in fact the sweetness of the Hereafter. Similarly, the sweet aspects of this world are in fact exactly the bitter aspects of this world. This is because the person moving from a bitterness that is temporary to a sweetness that is eternal is much better for him than the opposite. If this truth is obscure to you, consider what the most truthful speaker [the Prophet Muhammad (peace be upon him)] has said,

حُفَّتِ الْجَنَّةُ بِالْمَكَارِه وَحُفَّتِ النَّارُ بِالشَّهَوَات

"Paradise has been surrounded by hardships while the Fire is surrounded by desires." (Recorded by Muslim.)

(13) If a person hears of the death of one of the enemy's of Islam, he should say,

الْحَمْدُ لِلَّهِ الَّذِي نَصَرَ عَبْدَهُ وَأَعَزَّ دِينَهُ

"All praise are due to Allah who gave victory to His servant and gave strength to his religion." (Recorded by ibn al-Sunee.[1])

(14) It is not allowed to wail over the deceased. The Messenger of Allah (peace be upon him) said,

لَيْسَ مِنَّا مَنْ لَطَمَ الْخُدُودَ وَشَقَّ الْجُيُوبَ وَدَعَا بِدَعْوَى الْجَاهِلِيَّةِ

"He is not one of us who scratches the cheek, rips the garment and makes the calls of the times of Ignorance.[2]" (Recorded by al-Bukhari.) The Messenger of Allah (peace be upon him) declared himself free of those people who wail over death, shave their heads due to an affliction or tear apart their clothing at such times. (Recorded by Muslim.) As for light crying without wailing or moaning, such is permissible. The Messenger of Allah (peace be upon him) said,

إِنَّ اللَّهَ لَا يُعَذِّبُ بِدَمْعِ الْعَيْنِ وَلَا بِحُزْنِ الْقَلْبِ وَلَكِنْ يُعَذِّبُ بِهَذَا

وَأَشَارَ إِلَى لِسَانِهِ أَوْ يَرْحَمُ

"Verily, Allah does not punish for the tears of the eye or for the grieving of the heart. But He punishes for this," and he pointed to his tongue, "or He shows mercy." (Recorded by al-Bukhari.)

(15) When performing the Funeral Prayer, after the second *takbeer* (saying of *Allahu akbar*), one should say the following,

اللَّهُمَّ اغْفِرْ لِحَيِّنَا وَمَيِّتِنَا وَشَاهِدِنَا وَغَائِبِنَا وَصَغِيرِنَا وَكَبِيرِنَا وَذَكَرِنَا

وَأُنْثَانَا

---

1 According to al-Salafi and al-Hilaali, this hadith is weak. See al-Salafi, p. 198; al-Hilaali, vol. 1, p. 392.—JZ

2 The calls of the times of Ignorance include any deed that was acted upon during the time of Ignorance and which is considered repugnant or forbidden in Islam. In fact, every deed that goes against what the Messenger of Allah (peace be upon him) brought is an act of the time of Ignorance.

"O Allah, forgive those of us alive and those dead, those present of us and those not present, the young of us and the elderly, and our males and our females.[1]" [Recorded by al-Tirmidhi.[2]]

اللَّهُمَّ اغْفِرْ لَهُ وَارْحَمْهُ وَعَافِهِ وَاعْفُ عَنْهُ وَأَكْرِمْ نُزُلَهُ وَوَسِّعْ مُدْخَلَهُ وَاغْسِلْهُ بِالْمَاءِ وَالثَّلْجِ وَالْبَرَدِ وَنَقِّهِ مِنَ الْخَطَايَا كَمَا نَقَّيْتَ الثَّوْبَ الْأَبْيَضَ مِنَ الدَّنَسِ وَأَبْدِلْهُ دَارًا خَيْرًا مِنْ دَارِهِ وَأَهْلاً خَيْرًا مِنْ أَهْلِهِ وَزَوْجًا خَيْرًا مِنْ زَوْجِهِ وَأَدْخِلْهُ الْجَنَّةَ وَأَعِذْهُ مِنْ عَذَابِ الْقَبْرِ وَ مِنْ عَذَابِ النَّارِ

"O Allah, forgive him; have mercy on him; pardon him and excuse him; give him an honorable reception; make his grave wide; wash him with water, snow and ice; cleanse him of sin as a white garment is cleansed of filth; exchange for him an abode that is better than his present abode, and his family for a better family and his spouse for a better spouse. Enter him into Paradise. Protect him from the punishment of the grave and the punishment of the Hell-fire.[3]" [Recorded by Muslim.]

If the deceased was a child, one should pray for its parents by saying,

اللَّهُمَّ اجْعَلْهُ لَنَا فَرَطًا وَسَلَفًا وَأَجْرًا

---

[1] *Dhikr #109: allaahumma-gfir lihayyinaa wa mayyitanaa wa shaahidinaa wa gaaṣibinaa wa sageerinaa wa kabeerinaa wa dhakarinaa wa ṣunthaanaa.*

[2] According to al-Albani, this hadith is *sahih*. See al-Albani, *Sahih Sunan al-Tirmidhi*, vol. 1, p. 299.—JZ

[3] *Dhikr #110: allahumma-gfir lahu warhamhu wa 'aafihi wa'fu 'anhu wa ṣakrim nuzulahu wa wassi' mudkhalahu wa-gsilhu bi-l-maṣi wa-l-thalji wa-l-baradi wa naqqihi mina-l-khataayaa kamaa naqqaita-thauba-l-ṣabyada mina-ddanasi wa ṣabdilhu daaran khairan min daarihi wa ahlan khairan min ahlihi wa zaujan khairan min zaujihi wa ṣadkhilhu-l-jannata wa ṣa'idhhu min 'adhaabi-l-qabri wa min 'adhaabi-nnaar.*

"O Allah, make him for us one who prepares the way for us and precedes us [for which we are deserving reward] and a source of reward." (Recorded by al-Bukhari.[1])

One should also say,

اللّهمّ ثقل به موازينهما وأفرغ الصبر على قلوبهما ولا تفتنهما بعده ولا تحرمهما أجره

"O Allah, make their scales heavier due to him, pour patience over their hearts, do not try them after him and do not prevent them from his reward."[2]

The Prophet (peace be upon him) used to order the people to have sincerity in their supplications for the deceased. (Recorded by Abu Dawood.[3])

(16) When placing the deceased in the grave, one should say,

بِسْمِ اللهِ وَعَلَى سُنَّةِ رَسُوْلِ اللهِ

"In the name of Allah and according to the sunnah of the Messenger of Allah.[4]" (Recorded by al-Tirmidhi.[5])

(17) After the deceased was buried, the Messenger of Allah (peace be upon him) would stand at his grave and say [to those with him],

اسْتَغْفِرُوا لِأَخِيكُمْ وَسَلُوا لَهُ بِالتَّثْبِيتِ فَإِنَّهُ الآنَ يُسْأَلُ

---

[1] Actually, al-Bukhari only recorded this in *mualiq* form (meaning, without a complete chain) and, furthermore, he recorded it only as an act of al-Hasan al-Basri and not that of the Prophet (peace be upon him). According to ibn Hajr, the complete chain of this report back to al-Hasan only may be found in Abdul Wahaab ibn Ata's book *al-Janaaiz*. See Ahmad ibn Hajr, *Fath al-Bari bi-Sharh Sahih al-Bukhari* (Beirut: Dar al-Fikr, 1993), vol. 3, p. 564.—JZ

[2] Until now, this translator could not find a source for this supplication and the author himself did not mention any source. Allah knows best.—JZ

[3] According to al-Albani, this hadith is *hasan*. See al-Albani, *Sahih Sunan Abi Dawood*, vol. 2, pp. 616-617.—JZ

[4] *Dhikr* #111: *bismilaahi wa 'alaa-ssunnati rasooli-laah.*

[5] According to al-Albani, this hadith is *sahih*. See al-Albani, *Sahih Sunan Abi Dawood*, vol. 2, p. 619.—JZ

"Seek forgiveness for your brother and ask for him to be given firmness and constancy for he is now being questioned." (Recorded by Abu Dawood.[1])

(18) Upon giving condolences to the family of the deceased, one should say,

$$إِنَّ لِلَّهِ مَا أَخَذَ وَلَهُ مَا أَعْطَى وَكُلٌّ عِنْدَهُ بِأَجَلٍ مُسَمَّى$$

"To Allah belongs what He took, to Him belongs what He gave and everything has a prescribed time with Him.[2]" (Recorded by al-Bukhari.)

(19) Upon visiting gravesites or cemeteries, one should say,

$$السَّلامُ عَلَيْكُمْ أَهْلَ الدِّيَارِ مِنَ الْمُؤْمِنِينَ وَالْمُسْلِمِينَ وَإِنَّا إِنْ شَاءَ اللَّهُ$$

$$لاحِقُونَ أَسْأَلُ اللَّهَ لَنَا وَلَكُمُ الْعَافِيَةَ$$

"Peace be upon you, o inhabitants of the graves from believers and Muslims. We, Allah willing, shall be joining you. I ask Allah for us and for you well-being.[3]" (Recorded by Muslim.)

(20) It is prohibited to visit the lands of the people who were destroyed by Allah. If one must pass through such lands, he should do so in fear and crying. The Prophet (peace be upon him) told his Companions when they had reached the land of the people of Thamood,

$$لا تَدْخُلُوا عَلَى هَؤُلاءِ الْمُعَذَّبِينَ إِلاَّ أَنْ تَكُونُوا بَاكِينَ فَإِنْ لَمْ تَكُونُوا$$

$$بَاكِينَ فَلا تَدْخُلُوا عَلَيْهِمْ لا يُصِيبُكُمْ مَا أَصَابَهُمْ$$

"Do not enter upon [the lands of] those who were punished except in a state of crying. If you do not cry, then do not enter

---

[1] According to al-Albani, this hadith is *sahih*. See al-Albani, *Sahih Sunan Abi Dawood*, vol. 2, p. 620.—JZ

[2] *Dhikr* #112: *ϵinna lilaahi maa ϵakhadha wa lahu maa ϵa'taa wa kullun 'indahu bi ϵajalin musamma.*

[3] *Dhikr* #113: *as-salaamu 'alaikum ϵahla-ddiyaari mina-l-mu ϵmineena wa-l-muslimeena wa ϵinnaa ϵin shaa ϵa-llaahu laahiqoona ϵas ϵalu-llaaha lanaa wa lakumu-l-'aafiyah.*

upon them so that the same thing that afflicted them does not afflict you." (Recorded by al-Bukhari.)

Note: Every Muslim must realize that it is not allowed to honor any grave in a matter other than what has been stated in the texts. It is not allowed, for example, to have special visits to the grave, or to raise the grave more than a handspan above the ground; it is also prohibited to walk or sit upon the graves as well as walk among them while wearing sandals. It is not allowed to honor them by building structures over them, put tiles on them, put lamps over them, place flowers over them, wipe them to get blessings from them, seek blessings from their soil or any other act that may be a means to associating partners with Allah and concerning which the Messenger of Allah (peace be upon him) gave us a very strong warning.

Aisha narrated that during the last moments of the Prophet's life, he would cover his face with this shirt. When he felt hot, he would uncover his face and he said,

لَعْنَةُ اللَّهِ عَلَى الْيَهُودِ وَالنَّصَارَى اتَّخَذُوا قُبُورَ أَنْبِيَائِهِمْ مَسَاجِدَ

"The curse of Allah be upon the Jews and the Christians. They took the graves of their prophets as places of worship." He said this as a warning against what they had done. (Recorded by al-Bukhari and Muslim.) If it were not for his warnings, his grave would have been made a prominent place but they feared that it would be taken as a place of worship. The Messenger of Allah (peace be upon him) also said,

أَلَا وَإِنَّ مَنْ كَانَ قَبْلَكُمْ كَانُوا يَتَّخِذُونَ قُبُورَ أَنْبِيَائِهِمْ وَصَالِحِيهِمْ

مَسَاجِدَ أَلَا فَلَا تَتَّخِذُوا الْقُبُورَ مَسَاجِدَ إِنِّي أَنْهَاكُمْ عَنْ ذَلِكَ

"Certainly, those people who came before you used to take the graves of their prophets and righteous people as places of prayer. Beware, do not take the graves as places of prayer. I forbid that for you." (Recorded by Muslim.)

Jabir stated that the Prophet (peace be upon him) forbade the plastering of graves, sitting upon the graves and building of structures upon them. (Recorded by Muslim.)

(17) Words of Remembrance Related to Travel

(1) It is preferred to leave for one's travel on a Thursday and to leave early in the morning. (Recorded by al-Bukhari and Abu Dawood.)

(2) It is recommended for the person to pray two *rakats* before he leaves on his journey. This is based on the following hadith,

ما خلف عبد أهله أفضل من ركعتين يركعهما عندهم حين يريد

السفر

"A servant [of Allah] does not leave anything better behind for his family than two *rakats* that he prays with them at the time he is going to travel." (Recorded by al-Tabaraani.[1])

(3) When the traveler mounts or boards his means of transportation, he should say,

الله أَكْبَرُ الله أَكْبَرُ الله أَكْبَرُ سُبْحَانَ الَّذِي سَخَّرَ لَنَا هَذَا وَمَا كُنَّا لَهُ

مُقْرِنِينَ وَإِنَّا إِلَى رَبِّنَا لَمُنْقَلِبُونَ اللَّهُمَّ إِنَّا نَسْأَلُكَ فِي سَفَرِنَا هَذَا الْبِرَّ

وَالتَّقْوَى وَمِنَ الْعَمَلِ مَا تَرْضَى اللَّهُمَّ هَوِّنْ عَلَيْنَا سَفَرَنَا هَذَا وَاطْوِ عَنَّا

بُعْدَهُ اللَّهُمَّ أَنْتَ الصَّاحِبُ فِي السَّفَرِ وَالْخَلِيفَةُ فِي الْأَهْلِ اللَّهُمَّ إِنِّي أَعُوذُ

بِكَ مِنْ وَعْثَاءِ السَّفَرِ وَكَآبَةِ الْمَنْظَرِ وَسُوءِ الْمُنْقَلَبِ فِي الْمَالِ وَالْأَهْلِ

وَمِنَ الْحَوْرِ بَعْدَ الْكَوْنِ وَمِنْ دَعْوَةِ الْمَظْلُومِ

"Allah is greatest. Allah is greatest. Allah is greatest. Perfect is He who subjugated this for us and we ourselves would not have been capable of that. And our final journey is to our Lord. O Allah, we ask of You in this travel for piety and righteousness and for deeds that are pleasing to you. O Allah, make this traveling easy for us and make the distance shortened for us. O Allah, You are the Companion during the

---

[1] According to al-Hilaali, this hadith is *hasan* due to its supporting evidence. See al-Hilaali, vol. 1, pp. 546-547.—JZ

travel and the One who is left behind with the family. O Allah, I seek refuge in You from the hardship of travel, from seeing what is displeasing to me [occur to my family or wealth], from an ill-fated outcome for the wealth or family, and from *al-haur* after *al-kaur*[1] and from the supplication of the one who is wronged.[2]" (Recorded by Muslim and al-Tirmidhi.)

(4) When saying farewell to the one who is leaving, one should say,

$$أَسْتَوْدِعُ اللَّهَ دِينَكَ وَأَمَانَتَكَ وَخَوَاتِيمَ عَمَلِكَ$$

"I entrust your religion, those you are in charge of and your final deeds to Allah.[3]" (Recorded by Abu Dawood.[4])

(5) The one leaving should respond with the following words,

$$أَسْتَوْدِعُكَ اللَّهَ الَّذِي لَا تَضِيعُ وَدَائِعُهُ$$

"I place you in the trust of Allah who never wrongs any trust.[5]" (Recorded by ibn al-Sunee.[6])

(6) It is recommended to supplicate to Allah during one's travel, based on the hadith,

---

1 This means either returning to disbelief after faith, disobedience after obedience or from good affairs to evil ones.

2 *Dhikr* #114: *allaahu ¢akbar. allaahu ¢akbar. allaahu ¢akbar. subhaana-lladhee sakhara lanaa hadhaa wa maa kunna lahu muqrineena wa ¢innaa ¢ilaa rabbinaa lamunqaliboon. Allaahumma ¢innaa nas¢aluka fee safarinaa hadha-l-birra wa-ttaqwaa wa mina-l-'amali maa tardaa allaahumma hawwina 'alainaa safarinaa hadhaa wa-twi 'annaa bu'dahu allaahumma ¢anta-saahibu fee-safari wa-l-khaleefatu fee-l-ahli allaahumma ¢innee ¢a'oodhu bika min wa'tha ¢i-ssafari wa kaabati-l-mandari wa soo ¢i-munqalabi fee-l-maali wa-l-¢ahli wa mina-l-hauri ba'da-l-kauni wa min da'wati-l-madloom.*

3 *Dhikr* #115: *¢astaudi'u-llaaha deenaka wa ¢amaanataka wa khawaateema 'amalika.*

4 According to al-Hilaali, this hadith is *sahih* due to supporting evidence. See al-Hilaali, vol. 1, p. 551.—JZ

5 *Dhikr* #116: *¢astaudi'uka-llaaha-lladhee laa tadee'u wadaa ¢i'uhu.*

6 According to al-Hilaali, this hadith is *sahih* due to supporting evidence. See al-Hilaali, vol. 1, p. 550.—JZ

ثَلاثُ دَعَوَاتٍ مُسْتَجَابَاتٌ لا شَكَّ فِيهِنَّ دَعْوَةُ الْوَالِدِ وَدَعْوَةُ الْمُسَافِرِ وَدَعْوَةُ الْمَظْلُومِ

"There are three supplications that are responded to without any doubt concerning them: the supplication of the father, the supplication of the traveler and the supplication of the one who is wronged." (Recorded by Abu Dawood.[1])

(7) Upon ascending one should say, "*Allahu akbar*" ("Allah is greatest"). While descending, one should say, "*Subhaanallaah*" ("How perfect is Allah"). (Recorded by al-Bukhari.)

(8) If a traveler's means of transportation or animal should slip, he should say, "*Bismilaah*" ("In the name of Allah"). (Recorded by Abu Dawood.[2])

(9) If a person's animal escapes to the open spaces, one should call out, "O servants of Allah, capture him. O servants of Allah, capture him." (Recorded by ibn al-Sunee.[3])

(10) Upon seeing a city or town that the person wants to enter, he should say,

اللهُمَّ رَبَّ السَّمَوَاتِ السَّبْعِ وَمَا أَظْلَلْنَ وَالأَرَاضِينَ السَّبْعِ وَمَا أَقْلَلْنَ وَرَبَّ الشَّيَاطِينِ وَمَا أَضْلَلْنَ وَرَبَّ الرِّيَاحِ وَمَا ذَرَيْنَ أَسْأَلُكَ خَيْرَ هَذِهِ القَرْيَةِ وَخَيْرَ أَهْلِهَا وَخَيْرَ مَا فِيهَا وَنَعُوْذُ بِكَ مِنْ شَرِّهَا وَشَرِّ أَهْلِهَا وَشَرِّ مَا فِيْهَا

"O Allah, Lord of the seven heavens and what they shade, and of the seven earths and what they contain, and Lord of the devils and what they lead astray, and Lord of the winds and what they split asunder, I ask of You for the good of this

---

[1] According to al-Albani, this hadith is *hasan*. See al-Albani, *Sahih al-Jaami*, vol. 1, p. 582.—JZ

[2] According to al-Albani, this hadith is *sahih*. See al-Albani, *Sahih Sunan Abi Dawood*, vol. 3, p. 941.—JZ

[3] According to al-Hilaali, this hadith is very weak. See al-Hilaali, vol. 1, pp. 564-565.—JZ

town and the good of its people and the good of what it contains. And I seek refuge in You from its evil, the evil of its people and the evil it contains.[1]" (Recorded by al-Nasaai and ibn al-Sunee.[2])

(11) If the jinn of a land start to appear in front of a person, he should make the call to prayer. (Recorded by ibn al-Sunee.[3]) By this means, he will be able to repel its evil by the call to prayer because Satan turns away and flees when the call to prayer is made.

(12) When a person stops at a place, he should say,

أَعُوذُ بِكَلِمَاتِ اللَّهِ التَّامَّاتِ مِنْ شَرِّ مَا خَلَقَ

"I seek refuge in Allah's perfect words from the evil that He created.[4]" In that case, nothing will harm him until he leaves from that place. (Recorded by Muslim.)

(13) If nighttime falls while the person is traveling, he should say,

يَا أَرْضُ رَبِّي وَرَبُّكِ اللَّهُ أَعُوذُ بِاللَّهِ مِنْ شَرِّكِ وَشَرِّ مَا فِيكِ وَشَرِّ مَا خُلِقَ فِيكِ وَمِنْ شَرِّ مَا يَدِبُّ عَلَيْكِ وَأَعُوذُ بِاللَّهِ مِنْ أَسَدٍ وَأَسْوَدَ وَمِنَ الْحَيَّةِ وَالْعَقْرَبِ وَمِنْ سَاكِنِ الْبَلَدِ وَمِنْ وَالِدٍ وَمَا وَلَدَ

"O earth, my Lord and your Lord is Allah. I seek refuge in Allah from your evil, the evil that you contain, the evil that was created in you and from the evil of what crawls upon

---

[1] *Dhikr* #117: *allaahumma rabba-ssamaawaati-ssab'i wa maa ṣadlalna wa-l-ṣaraadeena-ssab'i wa maa ṣaqlalna wa rabba-shayaateeni wa maa ṣadlalna wa rabba-riyaabi wa maa dharaina ṣas ṣaluka khaira hadhihi-l-qaryati wa khaira ṣablihaa wa khaira maa feehaa wa ṣa'oodhu bika min sharrihaa wa sharri ṣablihaa wa sharri maa feehaa.*

[2] Actually, this hadith was not recorded by al-Nasaai in what is commonly known as *Sunan al-Nasaai*, which is what the author's statement would imply. It was recorded by al-Nasaai in *al-Sunan al-Kubra* and *Amal al-Yaum wa al-Lailah*. According to al-Hilaali, this hadith is *sahih*. See al-Hilaali, vol. 1, pp. 566-567.—JZ

[3] According to al-Hilaali, the hadith mentioning such is weak. See al-Hilaali, vol. 1, pp. 568-560.—JZ

[4] *Dhikr* #118: *ṣa'oodhu bikalimaati-laahi-ttaammaati min sharri maa khalaq.*

you. I seek refuge in Allah from lions, large black snakes, other snakes, scorpions, the jinn who inhabit this land and from one who begets and what he has begotten." (Recorded by Abu Dawood.[1])

(14) Upon returning from one's journey, one should say the same words that he said upon leaving with the following additional words,

آيِبُونَ تَائِبُونَ عَابِدُونَ لِرَبِّنَا حَامِدُونَ

"We are relenting, repenting, worshipping and praising our Lord.[2]" The person should first go to the mosque and pray two *rakats*. And he should not return to his wife during the nighttime.[3] (Recorded by al-Bukhari and Muslim.)

(15) It is recommended to say to one who is returning from the pilgrimage,

قَبِلَ اللهُ حَجَّكَ وَغَفَرَ ذَنْبِكَ وَأَخْلَفَ نَفَقَتَكَ

"Allah accept your pilgrimage, forgive your sins and replace what you have spent." (Recorded by al-Haakim.[4])

(18) Words of Remembrance Related to Eating and Drinking

(1) The Messenger of Allah (peace be upon him) would never eat while reclining, as he said,

لَا آكُلُ مُتَّكِئًا

---

[1] According to al-Albani and al-Hilaali, this hadith is weak. See al-Albani, *Dhaeef Sunan Abi Dawood*, p. 255; al-Hilaali, vol. 1, p. 570.—JZ

[2] *Dhikr* #119: *Aayiboona taa eiboona 'aabidoona lirabbinaa haamidoon.*

[3] He should not return to her at night in order that he does not come upon her at a time when she is not prepared to see him, when she has not shaved herself or cleaned herself. However, if it is first possible for him to inform her that such is when he is coming, then there is no harm in it.

[4] According to al-Hilaali, this hadith is weak. See al-Hilaali, vol. 1, p. 576. Al-Salafi also mentioned that its chain is weak. See al-Salafi, p. 178.—JZ

"I do not eat while reclining." (Recorded by al-Bukhari.) However, he would eat while sitting on his buttocks with his shins straight up.[1] The word "reclining" above has been explained to mean either to sit cross-legged or to be leaning or resting upon something like a pillar or something of that nature. It has also been explained to mean being on one's side. All of those types of sitting have some resemblance to the manners of the arrogant and haughty, which are not becoming the nature of servitude. The Prophet (peace be upon him) would eat with his three fingers. In this way, it prevents one from eating too much or being gluttonous.

From the Prophet's guidance is that he would drink while sitting. This was his normal custom. Perhaps he drank standing on some occasions. He would breathe twice or thrice while drinking.[2]

(2) When the food was presented to him, he would say,

اللهم بارك لنا فيما رزقتنا وقنا عذاب النار بسم الله

"O Allah, bless us in what You have provided for us and save us from the punishment of the Hell-fire. In the name of Allah." Then he would eat what was close to him and with his right hand. (Recorded by al-Bukhari and ibn al-Sunee.[3])

(3) When one forgets to mention the name of Allah at the outset of eating and remembers it while eating, he should say,

---

[1] This is the explanation of *al-iqaa* as given by the author. Another explanation is to sit on one's buttocks while having one's shins and thighs spread out in front of him. See Sayyid ibn Abbaas al-Jaleemi's footnotes to Muhammad ibn Isa al-Tirmidhi, *al-Shamaail al-Muhammadiyyah wa al-Khasaail al-Mustafiyyah* (Beirut: Muasassah al-Kutub al-Thaqafiyyah, 1992), p. 125. Allah knows best.—JZ

[2] Ibn al-Qayyim, *Zaad al-Maad*, vol. 4.

[3] Again, the author has combined some supplications and at the end of them simply said, for example, "Recorded by al-Bukhari and ibn al-Sunee." In this particular case, the words, "O Allah, bless... In the name of Allah," are from ibn al-Sunee. That particular hadith is weak according to al-Hilaali. (See al-Hilaali, vol. 2, p. 579.) Al-Bukhari has recorded that one should mention the name of Allah, eat with one's right hand and eat what is closest to the person.—JZ

بِسْمِ اللّهِ أَوَّلِهِ وَآخِرِهِ

"In the name of Allah over the beginning of it and the end of it.[1]" (Recorded by al-Tirmidhi.[2])

(4) Upon finishing one's food, one should say,

الْحَمْدُ لِلّهِ كَثِيرًا طَيِّبًا مُبَارَكًا فِيهِ غَيْرَ مَكْفِيٍّ وَلَا مُوَدَّعٍ وَلَا مُسْتَغْنًى

عَنْهُ رَبَّنَا

"All praise be to Allah, with an abundant, excellent, blessed praise, a never ending praise, which has no farewell to it, a praise that cannot be done without. He is Our Lord.[3]" (Recorded by al-Bukhari.)

(5) Upon drinking milk, the Messenger of Allah (peace be upon him) would say,

اللَّهُمَّ بَارِكْ لَنَا فِيهِ وَزِدْنَا مِنْهُ

"O Allah, bless us by it and increase it for us.[4]" (Recorded by Abu Dawood.[5])

(6) One should never mention any shortcoming in the food or drink. A hadith states, "The Messenger of Allah (peace be upon him) never mentioned any shortcoming in the food. If he desired something, he would eat it. If he disliked it, he would leave it." (Recorded by al-Bukhari.)

---

[1] *Dhikr* #120: *bismilaahi ʿawwalihi wa aakhirihi.*

[2] According to al-Hilaali, this hadith is *sahih* due to its supporting evidence. See al-Hilaali, vol. 2, pp. 580-581.—JZ

[3] *Dhikr* #121: *al-hamdulilaahi katheeran tayyiban mubaarakan feehi gaira makfiyyin wa laa muwadda'in wa laa mustagnan 'anhu rabbanaa.*

[4] *Dhikr* #122: *allaahumma baarik lanaa feehi wa zidnaa minhu.*

[5] According to al-Albani, this hadith is *hasan.* See *Sahih Sunan Abi Dawood,* vol. 2, p. 711.—JZ

(19) Words of Remembrance Related to Marriage and Connected Matters

(1) Upon congratulating a newlywed, it is recommended to say,

بَارَكَ اللّٰهُ لَكَ وَبَارَكَ عَلَيْكَ وَجَمَعَ بَيْنَكُمَا فِي خَيْرٍ

"Allah's blessing for you and His blessings upon you and may He join you together in goodness.[1]" (Recorded by Abu Dawood.[2]) One should not say, "May you have abundance and many children," [as this was what was said during the Times of Ignorance].

(3) When the man goes to his wife on the wedding night, he should say,

اللّٰهُمَّ إِنِّي أَسْأَلُكَ خَيْرَهَا وَخَيْرَ مَا جَبَلْتَهَا عَلَيْهِ وَأَعُوذُ بِكَ مِنْ شَرِّهَا
وَمِنْ شَرِّ مَا جَبَلْتَهَا عَلَيْهِ

"O Allah, I ask of You for its good and the good of what You have made it incline towards. And I seek refuge in You from its evil and the evil You have made it incline to.[3]" (Recorded by Abu Dawood.[4])

(3) At the time of sexual intercourse, one should say,

بِاسْمِ اللّٰهِ اللّٰهُمَّ جَنِّبْنَا الشَّيْطَانَ وَجَنِّبِ الشَّيْطَانَ مَا رَزَقْتَنَا

"In the name of Allah. O Allah, keep Satan away from us and keep Satan away from what You grant us.[5]" If it is

---

[1] *Dhikr* #123: *baaraka-llaahu laka wa baaraka 'alaika wa jama'a bainakumaa fee khair.*

[2] According to al-Albani, this hadith is *sahih*. See *Sahih Sunan Abi Dawood*, vol. 2, p. 400.—JZ

[3] *Dhikr* #124: *Allaahumma ¿innee ¿as¿aluka khairahaa wa khaira maa jabaltahaa 'alaihi wa ¿a'oodhu bika min sharrihaa wa min sharri maa jabaltahaa 'alaih.*

[4] According to al-Hilaali, this hadith is *hasan*. See al-Hilaali, vol. 2, p. 700.—JZ

[5] *Dhikr* #125: *bismilaahi allaahumma jannibnaa-shaitaana wa jannibi-shaitaana maa razaqtanaa.*

decreed that they should then have a child between them, Satan will never harm it. (Recorded by al-Bukhari.)

(4) During the woman's labor pains, she should often make the supplication related to times of distress and hardship. That supplication was mentioned earlier.

It is narrated that when it was close to the time for Faatimah to give birth, the Messenger of Allah (peace be upon him) ordered Umm Salamah and Zainab bint Jahsh to go to her and recite the "Verse of the Throne" and verse 54 of *Soorah al-Araaf* and to seek protection for her by reciting the last two chapters of the Quran over her. (Recorded by ibn al-Sunee.[1])

(5) When the child is born, it is recommended to say the call to prayer in the right ear and the *iqaama* in the left. (Recorded by Abu Dawood, ibn al-Sunee and al-Baihaqi.[2])

The secret behind that act, and Allah knows best, is for the first words that the child hears to be the statement of *tauheed* and the call to goodness. The child should be named on the seventh day and a good name should be chosen for the child. The *aqeeqah* should also be performed and he should be circumcised.

(20) Guarding One's Tongue

(1) Everyone must know that every responsible person must guard his tongue from every type of speech except that which contains some obvious benefit to it. If the benefit from not speaking is the same as that from speaking, then the *sunnah* (preferred act) is for one to remain silent. This is because such speech may lead one to what is forbidden or disliked. Indeed, this is usually the case. Being free of that

---

[1] According to both al-Hilaali and al-Salafi, this hadith is a fabricated hadith. See al-Hilaali, vol. 2, p. 703; al-Salafi, p. 219.—JZ

[2] It seems, Allah knows best, that all of the hadith supporting this practice are either weak, very weak or fabricated. See, for example, al-Hilaali, vol. 2, pp. 704-705.—JZ

offense has no equivalent to it. (From the words of al-Nawawi in *al-Adhkaar*.)

(2) Abu Musa al-Ashari narrated that the people said, "O Messenger of Allah, who is the most virtuous Muslim?" He answered,

مَنْ سَلِمَ الْمُسْلِمُونَ مِنْ لِسَانِهِ وَيَدِهِ

"The one from whose tongue and hand the Muslims are safe." (Recorded by al-Bukhari.)

(3) The Messenger of Allah (peace be upon him) said,

وَمَنْ كَانَ يُؤْمِنُ بِاللَّهِ وَالْيَوْمِ الآخِرِ فَلْيَقُلْ خَيْرًا أَوْ لِيَصْمُتْ

"Whoever believes in Allah and the Last Day should speak what is good or remain silent." (Recorded by al-Bukhari.)

(4) The Messenger of Allah (peace be upon him) also said,

مَنْ يَضْمَنْ لِي مَا بَيْنَ لَحْيَيْهِ وَمَا بَيْنَ رِجْلَيْهِ أَضْمَنْ لَهُ الْجَنَّةَ

"For the one who can guarantee for me what is between his two jawbones and his two legs,[1] I guarantee for him Paradise." (Recorded by al-Bukhari.)

(5) The Prophet (peace be upon him) also said,

مِنْ حُسْنِ إِسْلامِ الْمَرْءِ تَرْكُهُ مَا لا يَعْنِيهِ

"Part of the perfection of the person's Islam is his leaving that which is of no concern to him" (Recorded by al-Tirmidhi.[2])

(6) It is prohibited to speak too much. This is based on the Prophet's statement,

لا تُكْثِرُوا الْكَلامَ بِغَيْرِ ذِكْرِ اللَّهِ فَإِنَّ كَثْرَةَ الْكَلامِ بِغَيْرِ ذِكْرِ اللَّهِ قَسْوَةٌ لِلْقَلْبِ وَإِنَّ أَبْعَدَ النَّاسِ مِنَ اللَّهِ الْقَلْبُ الْقَاسِي

---

[1] In other words, his tongue and his private part. The meaning is that he keeps them from what is forbidden.

[2] This hadith is on the borderline between *hasan* and weak. However, most likely, it should be considered a weak hadith. This translator discussed it in detail in *Commentary on the Forty Hadith of al-Nawawi*, hadith #12.—JZ

"Do not speak too much without the remembrance of Allah. Certainly speaking too much without remembrance of Allah hardens the heart. And the people who are furthest from Allah are those with hardened hearts." (Recorded by al-Tirmidhi.[1])

(7) It is prohibited to openly voice evil. Allah has said,

◆ لَّا يُحِبُّ ٱللَّهُ ٱلْجَهْرَ بِٱلسُّوٓءِ مِنَ ٱلْقَوْلِ إِلَّا مَن ظُلِمَ وَكَانَ ٱللَّهُ سَمِيعًا عَلِيمًا

"Allah does not like the public mention of evil except by one who has been wronged. And Allah is ever hearing and knowing" (*al-Nisaa* 148). The meaning is that Allah does not like foul speech or the causing of harm by one's tongue. However, for the one who has been wronged, he may speak out in order to make his claims against the one who is wronging him and to mention the evil and wrong that has been done. The Prophet (peace be upon him) once said,

إن شر الناس عند الله منزلة يوم القيامة من تركه الناس اتقاء شره

"The worst of people in Allah's sight on the Day of Resurrection is the one whom people avoid in order to safeguard themselves from his evil." (Recorded by al-Bukhari.)

(8) The Messenger of Allah (peace be upon him) said,

هل يكب الناس في النار على وجوههم أو على مناخرهم إلا حصائد ألسنتهم

---

[1] According to al-Albani, this hadith is weak. See al-Albani, *Dhaeef al-Jaami*, p. 904.—JZ

"Is there anything that has people thrown on their faces— or he said on their noses— into the Fire except what their tongues reap?" (Recorded by al-Tirmidhi.[1])

(9) Allah has forbidden backbiting, which is to mention your brother in a way that he does not like. Allah says,

$$\text{وَلَا يَغْتَب بَّعْضُكُم بَعْضًا}$$

"Do not backbite one another" (al-Hujuraat 12). The Prophet (peace be upon him) himself said,

$$\text{إِنَّ مِنْ أَرْبَى الرِّبَا الِاسْتِطَالَةَ فِي عِرْضِ الْمُسْلِمِ بِغَيْرِ حَقٍّ}$$

"The greatest form of usury is to go to lengths in speaking about a Muslim's honor without due right." (Recorded by Abu Dawood.[2])

(10) The Prophet (peace be upon him) said,

$$\text{لَا يَدْخُلُ الْجَنَّةَ نَمَّامٌ}$$

"The tale-carrier shall not enter Paradise." (Recorded by al-Bukhari.) "Tale-carrying" is to spread people's speech from one to another in a way that causes harm and evil.

The actions that will protect one from the effects of the tale-carrier are the following:[3]

a) The person should not believe the tale-carrier because such a person is an evildoer and his reports are to be rejected.

b) The tale-carrier should be advised and shown that his actions are repugnant.

---

[1] This hadith is graded *sahih* by the hadith scholars. For details concerning its narration, see the translator's *Commentary on the Forty Hadith of al-Nawawi*, hadith #29.—JZ

[2] According to al-Albani, this hadith is *sahih*. See al-Albani, *Sahih Sunan Abi Dawood*, vol. 3, p. 923.—JZ

[3] Al-Nawawi, *al-Adhkaar*, Chapter on Tale-Carrying.

c) The tale-carrier should be hated for the sake of Allah if he refuses to accept the advise or if he continues to perform that evil act.

d) No evil thoughts should be had about the one who the tale-carrier has spoken about.

e) The person who heard the tale-carrier should not go and verify what has been said to him.

f) The person who heard the tale-carrier should not convey what he has heard in order for himself to avoid the sin of tale-carrying.

(11) It is prohibited to speak evil of or challenge another's lineage. The Prophet (peace be upon him) said,

اثْنَتَان فِي النَّاسِ هُمَا بِهِمْ كُفْرٌ الطَّعْنُ فِي النَّسَبِ وَالنِّيَاحَةُ عَلَى الْمَيِّتِ

"There are two acts among the people and they are [the acts of the people] of disbelief: challenging lineages and wailing over the dead." (Recorded by Muslim.)

(12) Every Muslim has a great aspect of inviolability with respect to his blood, life and wealth. During the Farewell Pilgrimage, during the speech on the Day of Sacrifice at Mina, the Prophet (peace be upon him) said,

إِنَّ دِمَاءَكُمْ وَأَمْوَالَكُمْ وَأَعْرَاضَكُمْ عَلَيْكُمْ حَرَامٌ كَحُرْمَةِ يَوْمِكُمْ هَذَا فِي

بَلَدِكُمْ هَذَا فِي شَهْرِكُمْ هَذَا

"Verily, your blood, your wealth and your honor are inviolable to you as the inviolability of this day of yours in this land of yours in this month of yours." (Recorded by al-Bukhari.)

(14) It is considered appropriate behavior for a Muslim to listen to his brother until he has finished his words and not to cut him off. Not applying this etiquette leads to hatred and anger since it gives the impression that one is not concerned with what his brother is saying. This also leads to great disputes, less benefit in communication and loss of valuable time.

(15) Disputes and lots of quarrels are prohibited. The Prophet (peace be upon him) said,

إِنَّ أَبْغَضَ الرِّجَالِ إِلَى اللَّهِ الْأَلَدُّ الْخَصِمُ

"The most hated of men to Allah is the quarrelsome,
argumentative one." (Recorded by al-Bukhari.) The
quarrelsome is the one who often gets into heated arguments
and debates. The argumentative one is the one who argues
with his friends and uses fallacious arguments while he is not
willing to accept the truth.

(16) The Messenger of Allah (peace be upon him)
cautioned against wrongdoing, as it is greatly forbidden. The
Prophet (peace be upon him) said,

اتَّقُوا الظُّلْمَ فَإِنَّ الظُّلْمَ ظُلُمَاتٌ يَوْمَ الْقِيَامَةِ

"Guard against wrongdoing for verily wrongdoing is
darkness on the Day of Resurrection." (Recorded by Muslim.)
The Prophet (peace be upon him) also said,

إِنَّ اللَّهَ لَيُمْلِي لِلظَّالِمِ حَتَّى إِذَا أَخَذَهُ لَمْ يُفْلِتْهُ قَالَ ثُمَّ قَرَأَ (وَكَذَلِكَ
أَخْذُ رَبِّكَ إِذَا أَخَذَ الْقُرَى وَهِيَ ظَالِمَةٌ إِنَّ أَخْذَهُ أَلِيمٌ شَدِيدٌ)

"Certainly, Allah gives respite to the wrongdoer until He takes
him and he does not get away." Then the Prophet (peace be
upon him) recited the verse, "And thus is the seizing of your
Lord when He seizes the cities while they are doing wrong.
Indeed, His seizing is painful and severe" [*Hood* 102].
(Recorded by al-Bukhari.)

(17) It is prohibited to laugh too much. This is based
on the Prophet's statement,

أَقِلَّ الضَّحِكَ فَإِنَّ كَثْرَةَ الضَّحِكِ تُمِيتُ الْقَلْبَ

"Reduce laughing for much laughter deadens the heart."
(Recorded in *Al-Adab al-Mufrad*.[1])

---

[1] This hadith was recorded by al-Bukhari in his work *al-Adab al-Mufrad* but not in
his *Sahih*. According to al-Albani, this hadith is *sahih*. See Muhammad Nasir al-Din
al-Albani, *Sahih al-Adab al-Mufrad li-l-Imaam al-Bukhaari* (al-Zarqaa, Jordan:
Dar al-Sideeq, 1994), p. 112.—JZ

(18) It is prohibited to be a witness for a contract involving interest. In fact, the Messenger of Allah (peace be upon him) cursed the witness. He stated,

لَعَنَ اللَّهُ آكِلَ الرِّبَا وَمُوكِلَهُ وَشَاهِدَهُ وَكَاتِبَهُ

"Allah has cursed the one who takes interest, pays interest, witnesses it or records it." (Recorded by al-Tirmidhi.[1])

(19) It is forbidden to give false testimony. Due to the greatness of this sin, Allah has mentioned it in conjunction with associating partners with Allah. Allah has said,

فَٱجْتَنِبُواْ ٱلرِّجْسَ مِنَ ٱلْأَوْثَنِ وَٱجْتَنِبُواْ قَوْلَ

ٱلزُّورِ

"So avoid the filth of the idols and avoid false statements" (*al-Hajj* 30). Allah has also forbidden the hiding or concealing of the testimony that one knows. Allah has said,

وَلَا تَكْتُمُواْ

ٱلشَّهَـٰدَةَ وَمَن يَكْتُمْهَا فَإِنَّهُۥ ءَاثِمٌ قَلْبُهُۥ وَٱللَّهُ بِمَا تَعْمَلُونَ عَلِيمٌ

"And do not conceal the testimony, for whoever conceals it, his heart is indeed sinful. And Allah is Knowledgeable of what you do" (*al-Baqara* 283).

(20) It is also prohibited to be boastful. Allah says,

وَلَا تُصَعِّرْ خَدَّكَ لِلنَّاسِ وَلَا تَمْشِ فِى ٱلْأَرْضِ مَرَحًا إِنَّ ٱللَّهَ لَا يُحِبُّ كُلَّ

مُخْتَالٍ فَخُورٍ

---

1 Al-Tirmidhi, as well as Muslim, have recorded hadith that state that the Prophet (peace be upon him) cursed all of the categories mentioned in the above hadith.—JZ

"And do not turn your cheek [in contempt] toward people and walk not through the earth exultantly. Indeed, Allah does not like anyone who is self-deluded and boastful" (*Luqmaan* 18). The Prophet (peace be upon him) also said,

إِنَّ اللَّهَ أَوْحَى إِلَيَّ أَنْ تَوَاضَعُوا حَتَّى لا يَفْخَرَ أَحَدٌ عَلَى أَحَدٍ

"Allah has revealed to me to be humble to one another to the extent that no one boasts over another." (Recorded by Muslim.)

(21) It is not allowed for one to have an evil joy when his brother is facing a hardship. The Prophet (peace be upon him) stated,

لا تُظْهِرِ الشَّمَاتَةَ لِأَخِيكَ فَيَرْحَمَهُ اللَّهُ وَيَبْتَلِيكَ

"Do not display a wicked joy at your brother's hardship as then Allah will show mercy to him and put you to trial." (Recorded by al-Tirmidhi.[1])

(22) It is prohibited to scorn or mock a Muslim. Allah says,

يَٰٓأَيُّهَا ٱلَّذِينَ ءَامَنُواْ لَا يَسْخَرْ قَوْمٌ مِّن قَوْمٍ عَسَىٰٓ أَن يَكُونُواْ خَيْرًا مِّنْهُمْ وَلَا نِسَآءٌ مِّن نِّسَآءٍ عَسَىٰٓ أَن يَكُنَّ خَيْرًا مِّنْهُنَّ وَلَا تَلْمِزُوٓاْ أَنفُسَكُمْ وَلَا تَنَابَزُواْ بِٱلْأَلْقَٰبِ بِئْسَ ٱلِٱسْمُ ٱلْفُسُوقُ بَعْدَ ٱلْإِيمَٰنِ وَمَن لَّمْ يَتُبْ فَأُوْلَٰٓئِكَ هُمُ ٱلظَّٰلِمُونَ

"O you who believe, do not let a people ridicule another people as they may be better than them; nor let any women ridicule other women as they may be better than them. And do not insult one another and do not call each other by [offensive] nicknames. Wretched is the name of disobedience

---

[1] According to al-Albani, this hadith is weak. See al-Albani, *Dhaeef al-Jaami*, p. 901.—JZ

after faith. And whoever does not repent, such are the wrongdoers" (*al-Hujuraat* 11).

(23) It is prohibited to continually remind a person of a favor that one has done for him. Allah says in the Quran,

$$ يَتَأَيُّهَا ٱلَّذِينَ ءَامَنُواْ لَا تُبْطِلُواْ صَدَقَتِكُم بِٱلْمَنِّ وَٱلْأَذَىٰ $$

"O you who believe, do not render void your acts of charity by reminders of it or harm" (*al-Baqara* 264). The Quranic commentators state that this means, "do not render void its reward."

(24) It is also prohibited and condemned for people to spread the secrets of their marital relations. The Prophet (peace be upon him) stated,

$$ إِنَّ مِنْ أَشَرِّ النَّاسِ عِنْدَ اللَّهِ مَنْزِلَةً يَوْمَ الْقِيَامَةِ الرَّجُلَ يُفْضِي إِلَى امْرَأَتِهِ $$

$$ وَتُفْضِي إِلَيْهِ ثُمَّ يَنْشُرُ سِرَّهَا $$

"From among the people with the most evil position in Allah's sight is a man who goes privately to his wife and she goes private to him and then he spreads her secret relations." (Recorded by Muslim.)

(25) It is prohibited to repel the orphan or the poor. Allah says,

$$ فَأَمَّا ٱلْيَتِيمَ فَلَا تَقْهَرْ ۝ وَأَمَّا ٱلسَّآئِلَ فَلَا تَنْهَرْ $$

"So as for the orphan, do not oppress [him]. And as for the petitioner [who seeks aid], do not repel [him]" (*al-Dhuhaa* 9-10).

(26) It is not allowed to swear by anything other than Allah, such as swearing by the Kaabah, the trust, one's parents, one's honor, life, the Prophet and so forth. The Prophet (peace be upon him) stated,

$$ مَنْ حَلَفَ بِغَيْرِ اللَّهِ فَقَدْ كَفَرَ أَوْ أَشْرَكَ $$

"Whoever swears by other than Allah has committed unbelief or associated partners [with Allah]." (Recorded by al-Tirmidhi.[1]) The Prophet (peace be upon him) also said,

مَنْ كَانَ حَالِفًا فَلْيَحْلِفْ بِاللَّهِ أَوْ لِيَصْمُتْ

"If one is going to swear, he must swear by Allah or remain silent." (Recorded by al-Bukhari.)

It is also disliked to swear often while making business transactions, even if the person is truthful in what he is swearing to. The Prophet (peace be upon him) stated,

إِيَّاكُمْ وَكَثْرَةَ الْحَلِفِ فِي الْبَيْعِ فَإِنَّهُ يُنَفِّقُ ثُمَّ يَمْحَقُ

"Avoid too much swearing in business transactions for it produces a quick sale but it removes its blessings." (Recorded by Muslim.)

(27) Among the most evil of sins and lewd behavior is lying. It has been forbidden in both the Quran and the sunnah. Among the pieces of evidence prohibiting it is the following verse,

وَلَا تَقْفُ مَا لَيْسَ لَكَ بِهِۦ عِلْمٌ إِنَّ ٱلسَّمْعَ وَٱلْبَصَرَ وَٱلْفُؤَادَ كُلُّ أُوْلَٰٓئِكَ كَانَ عَنْهُ مَسْـُٔولًا

"And do not pursue [or speak about] that of which you have no knowledge. Indeed, the hearing, the sight and the heart—about all those one will be questioned" (*al-Israa* 36).

Furthermore, the Prophet (peace be upon him) stated,

آيَةُ الْمُنَافِقِ ثَلَاثٌ إِذَا حَدَّثَ كَذَبَ وَإِذَا وَعَدَ أَخْلَفَ وَإِذَا اؤْتُمِنَ خَانَ

"The signs of a hypocrite are three: when he speaks, he lies; when he makes a promise, he breaks it; when he is given a trust, he betrays it." (Recorded by al-Bukhari.)

---

[1] According to al-Albani, this hadith is *sahih*. See al-Albani, *Sahih Sunan al-Tirmidhi*, vol. 2, p. 99.—JZ

The greatest type of lie is to falsely attribute something to Allah or the Messenger (peace be upon him). Allah has said,

وَيَوْمَ ٱلْقِيَـٰمَةِ تَرَى ٱلَّذِينَ كَذَبُواْ عَلَى ٱللَّهِ وُجُوهُهُم مُّسْوَدَّةٌ أَلَيْسَ فِى جَهَنَّمَ مَثْوًى لِّلْمُتَكَبِّرِينَ

"And on the Day of Resurrection you will see those who lied about Allah with their faces blackened. Is there not in Hell a residence for the arrogant?" (*al-Zumar* 60).

Included under that form of lying is to declare something permissible or impermissible without the requisite knowledge. Allah says,

وَلَا تَقُولُواْ لِمَا تَصِفُ أَلْسِنَتُكُمُ ٱلْكَذِبَ هَـٰذَا حَلَـٰلٌ وَهَـٰذَا حَرَامٌ لِّتَفْتَرُواْ عَلَى ٱللَّهِ ٱلْكَذِبَ إِنَّ ٱلَّذِينَ يَفْتَرُونَ عَلَى ٱللَّهِ ٱلْكَذِبَ لَا يُفْلِحُونَ

"And do not say about what your tongues have spoken of falsehood, 'This is lawful and that is unlawful,' to invent falsehood about Allah. Indeed, those who invent falsehood about Allah will not succeed" (*al-Nahl* 116). The Prophet (peace be upon him) has also said,

لا تكذبوا عليّ فإنه من كذب عليّ متعمداً فليتبوأ مقعده من النار

"Do not falsely attribute anything to me for anyone who intentionally falsely attributes anything to me shall take his own abode in the Hell-fire." (Recorded by al-Bukhari.) Based on that, it is obligatory to confirm what a person is narrating and one should not narrate everything he hears when he does not believe that it is truthful. The Prophet (peace be upon him) said,

كَفَى بِالْمَرْءِ كَذِبًا أَنْ يُحَدِّثَ بِكُلِّ مَا سَمِعَ

"It is enough of a lie for a person that he narrates everything
that he hears." (Recorded by Muslim.)

(21) Abusive Language and Cursing

(1) It is forbidden to revile the Companions of the
Prophet (peace be upon him). The Prophet himself said,

لا تَسُبُّوا أَصْحَابِي فَلَوْ أَنَّ أَحَدَكُمْ أَنْفَقَ مِثْلَ أُحُدٍ ذَهَبًا مَا بَلَغَ مُدَّ

أَحَدِهِمْ وَلا نَصِيفَهُ

"Do not revile my Companions. If one of you were to spend in
gold an amount equivalent to Mount Uhud it would not reach
[the virtue] of a handful or even half of that of one of them."
(Recorded by al-Bukhari.)

Al-Nawawi wrote, in his commentary to *Sahih
Muslim*, "Know that reviling a Companion is forbidden and is
one of the lewdest forbidden acts. This is true regardless of
whether the reviled Companion was one of those involved in
the civil strife or not. This is because they were *mujtahideen*
[those who strove their utmost to come to the correct
conclusion concerning that matter] in those battles and
interpreted the matters according to what they believed to be
correct." The punishment for the act of reviling a Companion
is mentioned in another hadith of the Prophet (peace be upon
him),

لعن الله من سبَّ أصحابي

"Allah curses whoever reviles my Companions." (Recorded by
al-Tabaraani.[1])

(2) It is forbidden to revile or curse a Muslim. The
Prophet has said,

---

[1] According to al-Albani, this hadith is *hasan*. See al-Albani, *Sahih al-Jaami*, vol. 2,
p. 909.—JZ

سِبَابُ الْمُسْلِمِ فُسُوقٌ وَقِتَالُهُ كُفْرٌ

"Abusing a Muslim is an iniquity and fighting against him is a
[minor form] of infidelity." (Recorded by al-Bukhari.) The
Prophet (peace be upon him) also said,

لَعْنُ الْمُؤْمِنِ كَقَتْلِه

"Cursing a believer is like killing him." (Recorded by al-
Bukhari.) Cursing is like a prayer to distance a person from
the mercy of Allah.

The Messenger of Allah (peace be upon him) also
said,

الْمُسْتَبَّانِ مَا قَالَا فَعَلَى الْبَادِئِ مَا لَمْ يَعْتَدِ الْمَظْلُومُ

"The two who revile each other are according to what they
say and it will be against the one who started it as long as the
one who was wronged does not go beyond the proper
limits." (Recorded by Abu Dawood.[1]) The meaning of this
hadith is that when two people revile or abuse each other, the
sin will be upon the one who started the cursing and reviling
as long as the one who has been wrongfully reviled does not
go beyond the limits by cursing the first person in a greater or
worse fashion than he was cursed.

When a person curses another, the curse itself may
return to him, as mentioned in a hadith,

مَنْ لَعَنَ شَيْئًا لَيْسَ لَهُ بِأَهْلٍ رَجَعَتِ اللَّعْنَةُ عَلَيْهِ

"Whoever curses something that does not behoove it, the
curse returns to him." (Recorded by al-Tirmidhi.[2])

It is permissible to curse sinners as a class so long as
a specific person is not singled out or identified. This is found
in numerous hadith, such as, "Allah's curse be on the one
who takes interest," "Allah's curse be one who curses his
parents," and "Allah's curse be on one who makes an animal

---

[1] Actually, the hadith was also recorded by Muslim.—JZ
[2] According to al-Albani, this hadith is *sahih*. See al-Albani, *Sahih Sunan al-Tirmidhi*, vol. 2, p. 189.—JZ

sacrifice for someone other than Allah." (Recorded by Muslim.)

(3) It is forbidden to curse time. The Prophet (peace be upon him) stated,

$$ لَا تَسُبُّوا الدَّهْرَ فَإِنَّ اللَّهَ هُوَ الدَّهْرُ $$

"Do not curse time for verily Allah is [the Controller] of time." (Recorded by Muslim.) The meaning of, "for verily Allah is the time," means that Allah is the one who is the doer of the actions and events that occur in time.

(4) It is forbidden to curse the wind. The Messenger of Allah (peace be upon him) stated,

$$ لَا تُسُبُّوا الرِّيحَ فَإِنَّهَا مِنْ رَوْحِ اللَّهِ تَأْتِي بِالرَّحْمَةِ وَالْعَذَابِ وَلَكِنْ سَلُوا $$
$$ اللَّهَ مِنْ خَيْرِهَا وَتَعَوَّذُوا بِاللَّهِ مِنْ شَرِّهَا $$

"Do not curse the wind for it is from the spirit [belonging to] Allah. It brings mercy and punishment. But ask Allah for its good and seek refuge in Allah from its evil." (Recorded by Muslim.[1])

(5) It is also prohibited to curse the dead.[2]

[(6) Do not curse disbelievers or what they worship in a way that will cause harm to believers.[3]] Allah says in the Quran,

$$ وَلَا تَسُبُّوا الَّذِينَ يَدْعُونَ مِنْ دُونِ اللَّهِ فَيَسُبُّوا اللَّهَ عَدْوًا بِغَيْرِ عِلْمٍ $$

"Do not insult those they invoke other than Allah lest they insult Allah in enmity without knowledge" (*al-Anaam* 108). The Prophet (peace be upon him) also said,

---

[1] It is stated in the text that this hadith is recorded by Muslim. However, that is most likely a typographical error. Instead, this hadith was recorded by ibn Maajah and Ahmad. According to al-Albani, this hadith is *sahih*. See al-Albani, *Sahih al-Jaami*, vol. 2, p. 1223.—JZ

[2] At this portion in the text, there seems to be some mistake. The passage that follows this sentence is completely irrelevant. Most likely, the author originally included the hadith, "Do not curse the dead." (Recorded by al-Bukhari.)—JZ

[3] This portion does not form part of the text but it or something similar to it is obviously what should have been stated here. Allah knows best.—JZ

لا تؤذوا مسلما بشتم كافر

"Do not harm a Muslim by abusing a disbeliever." (Recorded by al-Haakim.[1])

(7) There is no benefit in reviling Satan for he is already accursed. Instead, one must always seek refuge in Allah from his evil. It is stated in a hadith,

لا تسبوا الشيطان وتعوذوا بالله من شره

"Do not revile Satan but seek refuge in Allah from his evil."[2]

(8) It is also prohibited to curse a fever. The Prophet (peace be upon him) stated to Umm al-Saaib or Umm al-Musayyib,

لا تَسُبِّي الْحُمَّى فَإِنَّهَا تُذْهِبُ خَطَايَا بَنِي آدَمَ كَمَا يُذْهِبُ الْكِيرُ خَبَثَ الْحَدِيدِ

"Do not curse a fever for it removes the sins of humans like the furnace removes the alloy of iron." (Recorded by Muslim.)

(9) It is prohibited to curse the riding animal. In a hadith, it states that the Prophet (peace be upon him) was on a journey while one of the women of the Ansar was riding a camel. The woman got irked by the camel and cursed it. The Messenger of Allah (peace be upon him) heard that and said, "Take everything that is upon it and let it go [free] for it is accursed." Imran, the sub-narrator, said, "It is as if I am looking at it right now as it would walk among the people and no one would give it any attention." (Recorded by Muslim.) Included in this category is the cursing of the modern forms of transportation [such as one's car].

---

1 According to al-Albani, this hadith is *sahib*. See al-Albani, *Sahib al-Jaami*, vol. 2, p. 1207.—JZ

2 This hadith was recorded by al-Dailaami and Tamaam. According to al-Albani, this hadith is *sahib*. See al-Albani, *Sahib al-Jaami*, vol. 2, p. 1223.—JZ

(22) Some Reprehensible Terms

(1) The statement, "My soul has become evil."

(2) For one to say, "The people have been destroyed." If one says that, then he himself is ruined.

(3) The statement, "Whatever Allah wills and whatever so and so wills." Instead, one should say, "Whatever Allah wills and then whatever so and so wills." Similarly, one should not say, "If it were not for Allah and so and so." Instead, one should say, "If it were not for Allah and then so and so."

(4) The statement, "If I were to do that, I would be a Jew, Christian or free of Islam."

(5) It is forbidden to say to a Muslim, "O disbeliever."

(6) It is forbidden to say to a hypocrite, "O sir," or "O leader".

(7) It is forbidden for a woman to describe to her husband or to any other man the beauty of another woman's body.

(8) It is reprehensible to speak too much and at length without restricting oneself to what is beneficial and useful.

(9) It is reprehensible to ask common folk difficult questions and get them involved in such discussions with the purpose of making them confused and doubtful.

(10) It is not allowed to say that so and so is from the people of Paradise or that so and so is from the people of Hell. Similarly, it is not allowed to say, "May Allah not forgive you," and so forth. Allah has said,

فَلَا تُزَكُّوٓا۟ أَنفُسَكُمْ هُوَ أَعْلَمُ بِمَنِ ٱتَّقَىٰٓ

"Do not claim purity for yourselves; He knows best who is God-fearing" (*al-Najm* 32).

(11) The statement, "O frustration of time."

(23) Statements and Actions that are Prohibited for a Muslim

(1) One is ordered to fulfill pledges and fulfill promises. One must not spread about what is to be kept secret. Allah says,

$$وَأَوْفُوا بِالْعَهْدِ إِنَّ الْعَهْدَ كَانَ مَسْئُولًا$$

"And fulfill every commitment. Certainly, the commitments will be asked about" (al-Israa 34). Furthermore, the Prophet (peace be upon him) said,

أَرْبَعٌ مَنْ كُنَّ فِيهِ كَانَ مُنَافِقًا خَالِصًا. وَمَنْ كَانَتْ فِيهِ خَصْلَةٌ مِنْهُنَّ

كَانَتْ فِيهِ خَصْلَةٌ مِنَ النِّفَاقِ حَتَّى يَدَعَهَا إِذَا اؤْتُمِنَ خَانَ وَإِذَا حَدَّثَ

كَذَبَ وَإِذَا عَاهَدَ غَدَرَ وَإِذَا خَاصَمَ فَجَرَ

"There are four characteristics that if a person possesses all of them, he is a pure hypocrite. If he possesses any of them, then he possesses that characteristic of hypocrisy until he gives it up. [These four are:] if he is given a trust, he betrays it; when he speaks, he lies; when he makes a commitment, he breaks it; if he disputes, he is profligate." (Recorded by al-Bukhari.)

(2) It is forbidden to seek information from fortune-tellers and diviners. The Messenger of Allah (peace be upon him) stated,

مَنْ أَتَى عَرَّافًا فَسَأَلَهُ عَنْ شَيْءٍ لَمْ تُقْبَلْ لَهُ صَلاةٌ أَرْبَعِينَ لَيْلَةً

"For whoever goes to a fortune-teller to ask him about something, his prayers will not be accepted from him for forty nights." (Recorded by Muslim.) The Prophet (peace be upon him) also said,

مَنْ أَتَى كَاهِنًا أَوْ عَرَّافًا فَصَدَّقَهُ بِمَا يَقُولُ فَقَدْ كَفَرَ بِمَا أُنْزِلَ عَلَى

مُحَمَّدٍ

"Whoever goes to a diviner or a fortune-teller and believes in what he says, he then disbelieves in what was revealed to Muhammad." (Recorded by Ahmad and al-Haakim.[1])

Al-Nahawi stated, "The diviner is the one who claims to know about things that have happened in the past, such as guiding one to something which has been stolen or the place in which something has been lost. The fortune-teller is the one who talks about unseen events of the future. Both of these two groups claim to have some knowledge of the unseen. However, no one knows the unseen except Allah. Similar to those people are palm readers and tea leaf readers."

(3) It is not allowed to rule or judge not in accordance with what Allah has revealed. Allah says,

وَمَن لَّمْ يَحْكُم بِمَآ أَنزَلَ ٱللَّهُ فَأُوْلَٰٓئِكَ هُمُ ٱلْكَٰفِرُونَ

"Whoever rules not in accordance with what Allah has revealed, they certainly are the disbelievers" (*al-Maaidah* 44).

(4) It is not allowed to make a vow other than for the sake of Allah. The Prophet (peace be upon him) stated,

مَنْ نَذَرَ أَنْ يُطِيعَ اللَّهَ فَلْيُطِعْهُ وَمَنْ نَذَرَ أَنْ يَعْصِيَهُ فَلا يَعْصِهِ

"Whoever makes a vow to obey Allah, he should obey Him. Whoever vows to disobey Him, he should not disobey Him." (Recorded by al-Bukhari.)

In general, making vows is disapproved. The Messenger of Allah (peace be upon him) stated,

لا تَنْذِرُوا فَإِنَّ النَّذْرَ لا يُغْنِي مِنَ الْقَدَرِ شَيْئًا وَإِنَّمَا يُسْتَخْرَجُ بِهِ مِنَ الْبَخِيلِ

"Do not make vows for certainly vows do not avert Fate. They only take some wealth from the greedy." (Recorded by Muslim.) This is because the one who gives such money or

---

1 According to al-Albani, this hadith is *sahih*. See al-Albani, *Sahih al-Jaami*, vol. 2, p. 1031.—JZ

voluntary act due to an oath does not really do so voluntarily but his act is dependent on the result of what he took a vow concerning.

(5) It is one of the great sins to wrongfully accuse the Muslim men and women of illegal sexual intercourse. Allah says,

إِنَّ ٱلَّذِينَ يَرْمُونَ ٱلْمُحْصَنَٰتِ ٱلْغَٰفِلَٰتِ ٱلْمُؤْمِنَٰتِ لُعِنُواْ فِى ٱلدُّنْيَا وَٱلْأَخِرَةِ وَلَهُمْ عَذَابٌ عَظِيمٌ

"Indeed, those who [falsely] accuse chaste, unaware and believing women are cursed in this world and the Hereafter, and they will have a great punishment" (al-Noor 23).

(6) It is a must that a Muslim conceals his brother's faults. A hadith states,

لَا يَسْتُرُ عَبْدٌ عَبْدًا فِي الدُّنْيَا إِلاَّ سَتَرَهُ اللَّهُ يَوْمَ الْقِيَامَةِ

"No person conceals another's [faults] in this world except that Allah conceals his [faults] on the Day of Resurrection." (Recorded by Muslim.) It is not allowed to look into the private affairs of the Muslims and then to spread such matters about. Allah has said,

إِنَّ ٱلَّذِينَ يُحِبُّونَ أَن تَشِيعَ ٱلْفَٰحِشَةُ فِى ٱلَّذِينَ ءَامَنُواْ لَهُمْ عَذَابٌ أَلِيمٌ فِى ٱلدُّنْيَا وَٱلْأَخِرَةِ

"Indeed, those who like that immorality should be spread [or publicized] among those who believe will have a painful punishment in this world and the Hereafter" (al-Noor 19).

(7) It is not allowed for a Muslim to tear down the covering that Allah has put over his sins. The Prophet (peace be upon him) stated,

كُلُّ أُمَّتِي مُعَافًى إِلَّا الْمُجَاهِرِينَ وَإِنَّ مِنَ الْمُجَاهَرَةِ أَنْ يَعْمَلَ الرَّجُلُ
بِاللَّيْلِ عَمَلًا ثُمَّ يُصْبِحَ وَقَدْ سَتَرَهُ اللَّهُ عَلَيْهِ فَيَقُولَ يَا فُلَانُ عَمِلْتُ الْبَارِحَةَ
كَذَا وَكَذَا وَقَدْ بَاتَ يَسْتُرُهُ رَبُّهُ وَيُصْبِحُ يَكْشِفُ سِتْرَ اللَّهِ عَنْهُ

"All of my Nation will be forgiven except for those who publicize their sins. Publicizing includes the case where a person does something during the night and then in the morning, although Allah had concealed his act, he says, 'O so and so, last night I did such and such.' He spent the night being concealed by Allah and in the morning he uncovered Allah's covering from himself." (Recorded by al-Bukhari and Muslim.)

(8) It is forbidden to damage the relationship between a husband and wife. The Prophet (peace be upon him) stated,

لَيْسَ مِنَّا مَنْ خَبَّبَ امْرَأَةً عَلَى زَوْجِهَا

"One who makes a wife dislike her husband is not from us.[1]" (Recorded by Abu Dawood.[2])

(9) Condemned Innovations and Heresies: Every innovation in the religion is forbidden and a form of misguidance. The Prophet (peace be upon him) has stated,

إِيَّاكُمْ وَمُحْدَثَاتِ الأُمُورِ فَإِنَّ كُلَّ مُحْدَثَةٍ بِدْعَةٌ وَكُلَّ بِدْعَةٍ ضَلَالَةٌ

"Remain away from invented matters. Every invented matter is an innovation and every innovation is a misguidance." (Recorded by Abu Dawood.[3]) The Prophet (peace be upon him) also said,

مَنْ أَحْدَثَ فِي أَمْرِنَا هَذَا مَا لَيْسَ فِيهِ فَهُوَ رَدٌّ

---

[1] *Khabbab* means to ruin her. This is done by mentioning the shorcomings of the husband to the wife or by mentioning the excellent qualities of another man to her. (Taken from *Aoon al-Mabood*.)

[2] According to al-Albani, this hadith is *sahib*. See al-Albani, *Sahib al-Jaami*, vol. 2, p. 957.—JZ

[3] According to al-Albani, this hadith is *sahib*. See al-Albani, *Sahib al-Jaami*, vol. 3, p. 871.—JZ

"Whoever introduces a new matter into this affair of ours will have it rejected." (Recorded by al-Bukhari.)

These and other hadith indicate that every introduced matter in the religion is an innovation and a heresy. This means that every innovation in acts of worship or matters of belief is forbidden. However, the prohibition is of different levels depending on the type of innovation. Some such innovations are clear acts of disbelief, such as circumambulating graves, praying to people in the graves and seeking their help. Others are acts that are the means or stepping stones to associating partners with Allah, such as making supplications at grave sites.

There is no categorization of innovations into good one and bad ones. All innovations in the religion are evil and forms of straying from the truth. The following are among the factors that have led to the appearance of innovations:

a) Ignorance of the teachings of the religion itself.
b) Following desires and passions.
c) Blindly sticking to one way of life, custom or school.
d) Imitating the disbelievers.

(10) Omens: The Prophet (peace be upon him) said,

لا عَدْوَى وَلا طِيَرَةَ وَيُعْجِبُنِي الْفَأْلُ قَالُوا وَمَا الْفَأْلُ قَالَ كَلِمَةٌ طَيِّبَةٌ

"There is no contagiousness or bad omen. But I do like *al-fa'l* (a good omen)." They said, "What is *fa'l*?" He said, "A good word." (Recorded by al-Bukhari.)

A bad omen that is forbidden is where one acts or does not act due to that bad omen. However, if such a thought occurs to a person but he does not act upon it, it has no effect then on his belief. As for a good omen, it is like a good word, a pleasing sight, an act that one is pleased with, congratulations and so forth. A Muslim may take those as good indications. However, one cannot go beyond simply taking them as good signs. One must not put one's trust in them but one must, instead, place one's hopes in Allah and put one's trust in Him.

(11) Bribery: Giving bribes is one of the great sins. Thaubaan narrated,

لَعَنَ رَسُولُ اللّٰهِ صَلَّى اللّٰهِ عَلَيْهِ وَسَلَّمَ الرَّاشِيَ وَالْمُرْتَشِيَ وَالرَّائِشَ

"The Messenger of Allah (peace be upon him) cursed the one who gives a bribe, the one who takes a bribe and their intermediary." (Recorded by Ahmad.[1])

(12) Cutting off or not respecting the ties of kin. Allah says,

وَٱتَّقُواْ ٱللَّهَ ٱلَّذِى تَسَآءَلُونَ بِهِۦ وَٱلْأَرْحَامَ

"And fear Allah through whom you ask one another and [fear Him with respect to] the wombs [and ties of kin]" (al-Nisaa 1). The Prophet (peace be upon him) said,

لَا يَدْخُلُ الْجَنَّةَ قَاطِعُ رَحِمٍ

"One who cuts the ties of kinship will not enter Paradise." (Recorded by al-Bukhari.)

Keeping the proper ties of kinship leads to an increase in one's sustenance and a lengthening of one's life span. The Prophet (peace be upon him) said,

مَنْ أَحَبَّ أَنْ يُبْسَطَ لَهُ فِي رِزْقِهِ وَيُنْسَأَ لَهُ فِي أَثَرِهِ فَلْيَصِلْ رَحِمَهُ

"Whoever wishes to have his sustenance extended and have his lifetime extended should keep the ties of kinship." (Recorded by al-Bukhari.)

(13) Imitating others:

a) Imitating the Jews, Christians or other polytheists: Such an act is from the forbidden acts, regardless of whether the imitation is with respect to dress, customs or otherwise. This is based on the Prophet's statement,

---

[1] With this wording, the hadith is apparently weak. However, there are other hadith in which the Prophet (peace be upon him) stated, "Allah's curse be upon the one who gives a bribe and the one who takes a bribe concerning a judgment." (Recorded by Ahmad.) For more details, see Muhammad Naasir al-Deen al-Albani, *Ghaayat al-Maraam fi Takhreej Ahaadeeth al-Halaal wa al-Haraam* (Beirut: al-Maktab al-Islami, 1985), pp. 263-264.—JZ

مَنْ تَشَبَّهَ بِقَوْمٍ فَهُوَ مِنْهُمْ

"Whoever imitates [or appears] like a people is one of them."
(Recorded by Abu Dawood.[1]) Usually, the aspect that makes
one person imitate another is his being pleased with or
admiring of the other. This develops into love, mercy and
loyalty.

b) Men appearing like women and women appearing
like men: This is a lewd act that some people actually do. The
Messenger of Allah (peace be upon him) has cursed the
people who do such a thing. He has stated,

لَعَنَ اللَّهُ الْمُتَشَبِّهِينَ مِنَ الرِّجَالِ بِالنِّسَاءِ وَالْمُتَشَبِّهَاتِ مِنَ النِّسَاءِ

بِالرِّجَالِ

"Allah has cursed those men who appear like women and
those women who appear like men." (Recorded by Abu
Dawood.[2])

c) Imitating or appearing like animals: It is prohibited
for a Muslim to appear like an animal due to the differences
between the two. Allah has honored humans and
distinguished them. Hence, they should not imitate what is less
than them in appearance, character or nature.

(14) Singing and Music: Allah has forbidden singing
in the verse,

وَمِنَ ٱلنَّاسِ مَن يَشْتَرِى لَهْوَ ٱلْحَدِيثِ لِيُضِلَّ عَن سَبِيلِ ٱللَّهِ بِغَيْرِ

عِلْمٍ وَيَتَّخِذَهَا هُزُوًا أُوْلَٰٓئِكَ لَهُمْ عَذَابٌ مُّهِينٌ

"And of the people is he who buys the amusement of speech
to mislead [others] from the way of Allah without knowledge
and who takes it [His way] in ridicule. Those will have a

---

[1] According to al-Albani, this hadith is *sahih*. See al-Albani, *Sahih al-Jaami*, vol. 2, p. 1059.—JZ
[2] According to al-Albani, this hadith is *sahih*. See al-Albani, *Sahih al-Jaami*, vol. 2, p. 909.—JZ

humiliating punishment" (*Luqmaan* 6). The Quranic
commentators have stated that "the amusement of speech" is
singing. As for music, the Prophet (peace be upon him) has
mentioned it in the hadith,

لَيَكُونَنَّ مِنْ أُمَّتِي أَقْوَامٌ يَسْتَحِلُّونَ الْحِرَ وَالْحَرِيرَ وَالْخَمْرَ وَالْمَعَازِفَ

"There will be in my nation peoples who will try to make
illegal sexual intercourse, silk, alcohol and musical
instruments lawful." (Recorded by al-Bukhari.) In this hadith,
the Messenger of Allah (peace be upon him) stated musical
instruments and singing in association with illegal sexual
intercourse and alcohol. That is one of the clearest pieces of
evidence prohibiting singing and musical instruments.

(15) Ordering good and eradicating evil: The Nation
of the Prophet Muhammad (peace be upon him) is the best
nation due to its praiseworthy qualities. One of the most
important of those qualities is the ordering of good and
eradicating of evil. Allah has said,

كُـنتُمْ خَـيْرَ أُمَّـةٍ أُخْرِجَـتْ لِلنَّـاسِ تَـأْمُرُونَ بِـالْمَعْرُوفِ وَتَنْهَـوْنَ
عَـنِ الْمُنْكَـرِ وَتُؤْمِنُـونَ بِاللَّـهِ

"You are the best of nations produced for mankind. You order
what is good, eradicate what is evil and believe in Allah" (*ali-
Imraan* 110).

In this verse, Allah began by mentioning ordering
good and eradicating evil even before He mentioned faith
that is a prerequisite for the soundness of all acts of worship.
This shows how great that matter must be. Abandoning this
obligation leads to punishment and disaster. The Prophet
(peace be upon him) stated,

إِنَّ النَّاسَ إِذَا رَأَوُا الْمُنْكَرَ فَلَمْ يُنْكِرُوهُ أَوْشَكَ أَنْ يَعُمَّهُمُ اللَّهُ بِعِقَابِهِ

"Certainly if the people see an evil and they do not change it, Allah may soon inflict them all with His punishment." (Recorded by Ahmad.[1])

"Good" is everything that Allah and His Messenger have commanded. It includes all acts of obedience, those of speech as well as action. "Evil" is everything that Allah and His Messenger have prohibited. It includes all acts of disobedience, those of speech as well as action.

Removing evil is of different stages. A hadith states,

مَنْ رَأَى مِنْكُمْ مُنْكَرًا فَلْيُغَيِّرْهُ بِيَدِه فَإِنْ لَمْ يَسْتَطِعْ فَبِلِسَانِهِ فَإِنْ لَمْ

يَسْتَطِعْ فَبِقَلْبِهِ وَذَلِكَ أَضْعَفُ الإِيَمَان

"Whoever of you sees an evil must then change it with his hand. If he is not able to do so, then [he must change it] with his tongue. And if he is not able to do so, then [he must change it] with his heart. And that is the slightest [effect of] faith." (Recorded by Muslim.)

(24) Wills, Bequests and Charitable Endowments

(1) Wills and Bequests

A bequest is an instruction as to what should be done after one's death. It may include giving some of one's wealth in charity, marrying one's daughters, washing the deceased, prayers for the deceased, division of one-third of the wealth and so forth.

If some people have some rights over you, if you have some rights over others or if you wish to donate some of your wealth, you should write a will and bequest as quickly as

---

1 According to al-Albani, this hadith is *sahih*. See al-Albani, *Sahih al-Jaami*, vol. 1, p. 398.—JZ

possible. It is from the sunnah to write such a document as soon as possible. You may change it later if you will. However, you should realize that writing such a document will not bring about your end any sooner; in the same way, delaying its writing will not delay your end in any way.

Al-Bukhari recorded on the authority of ibn Umar that the Messenger of Allah (peace be upon him) stated,

$$ مَا حَقُّ امْرِئٍ مُسْلِمٍ لَهُ شَيْءٌ يُوصِي فِيهِ يَبِيتُ لَيْلَتَيْنِ إِلاَّ وَوَصِيَّتُهُ مَكْتُوبَةٌ عِنْدَهُ $$

"It is not right for a Muslim man who has something that he wants to bequest to pass two nights except that he has that bequest recorded with him." Ibn Umar added, "Not one night has passed since I heard the Messenger of Allah (peace be upon him) say that except that I have my will with me."

Bequests are of two types:

a) Obligatory: If a person owes somebody something or some right or he has a trust with him, then it is obligatory upon him to make that clear in detail.

b) Recommended: This is a bequest concerning less than one-third of one's wealth that is to be given to those who do not automatically receive shares. It could be distributed to charitable organizations, relatives, strangers or for any general or particular type of good.

When you write your will, show it to a person of knowledge so that he may explain to you its ruling. He will also then be able to witness it for you. Do not restrict yourself to limited acts, such as people sacrificing animals on your behalf, but make your bequest general enough to encompass all types of righteous and good deeds, especially those in which the benefit is most widespread.

(2) Charitable Endowments

This is where a person keeps possession of the capital or material of something but he lets its fruits, product and profits go for charitable causes.

Charitable endowments are very noble and fulfilling acts in life. It makes its owner very happy when he sees its good results. The Prophet (peace be upon him) was asked, "What is the best charity?" He answered,

أَنْ تَصَدَّقَ وَأَنْتَ صَحِيحٌ شَحِيحٌ تَخْشَى الْفَقْرَ وَتَأْمُلُ الْغِنَى وَلا تُمْهِلْ

حَتَّى إِذَا بَلَغَتِ الْحُلْقُومَ قُلْتَ لِفُلان كَذَا وَلِفُلان كَذَا وَقَدْ كَانَ لِفُلان

"It is when you give charity while you are healthy and desirous for more, fearing poverty and contemplating riches. Do not put it off until your soul reaches your throat and you see, 'Such and such should be given to so and so and such and such to so and so.' At that time, it already belongs to so and so." [Recorded by al-Bukhari.]

Jaabir said, "Everyone of the Companions of the Prophet (peace be upon him) who had some wealth had a charitable endowment."

The Muslim should eagerly seek to participate in this type of work. The Prophet (peace be upon him) stated,

إِذَا مَاتَ الإِنْسَانُ انْقَطَعَ عَنْهُ عَمَلُهُ إِلاَّ مِنْ ثَلاثَةٍ إِلاَّ مِنْ صَدَقَةٍ جَارِيَةٍ أَوْ

عِلْمٍ يُنْتَفَعُ بِهِ أَوْ وَلَدٍ صَالِحٍ يَدْعُو لَهُ

"When a human dies his deeds come to an end except for three: Except for a perpetual charity, knowledge by which benefit is accrued and a pious son who prays for him." (Recorded by Muslim.)

(25) Mention of Some Acts of Expiation

(1) The Expiation of One who Had Intercourse with His Wife during the Daytime of Ramadhaan

Abu Huraira said: While we were sitting with the Messenger of Allah (peace be upon him), a man came and said, "O Messenger of Allah, I have been destroyed." The Messenger of Allah (peace be upon him) asked him, "What is wrong with you?" He answered, "I had intercourse with my wife while I was fasting." The Messenger of Allah (peace be upon him) then said, "Can you free a slave?" The man answered, "No." He then asked him, "Can you fast two months consecutively?" The man answered, "No." Then he asked him, "Can you feed sixty poor people?" The man answered again, "No." The Prophet (peace be upon him) waited some time and then, while in that state, there came a big batch of dates that were given in charity. The Prophet (peace be upon him) stated, "Where is the questioner?" The man answered, "It is I." The Prophet (peace be upon him) said, "Take these [dates] and give them in charity." The man said, "To be given to a family poorer than I, o Messenger of Allah (peace be upon him)? By Allah, there is no family between the two black plains surrounding Madinah poorer than I." At that time, the Prophet (peace be upon him) laughed until his canine teeth showed. Then he said, "Feed it to your family." (Recorded by al-Bukhari and Muslim.)

He should make up that day that he broke, based on the Prophet's statement,

صوم يوماً مكانه

"Fast a day in its place." (Recorded by Abu Dawood.[1])

(2) The Expiation for *al-Dhihaar*[2]

Allah says in the Quran,

---

[1] That is not the exact wording in *Sunan Abu Dawood* but that is its meaning. According to al-Albani, that hadith is *sahih*. See al-Albani, *Sahih Sunan Abi Dawood*, vol. 2, p. 455.—JZ

[2] *Al-Dhihaar* is where a man says to his wife, "You are to me like my mother's back," "like my mother," or something similar to that.

وَٱلَّذِينَ يُظَٰهِرُونَ مِن نِّسَآئِهِمْ ثُمَّ يَعُودُونَ لِمَا قَالُوا فَتَحْرِيرُ رَقَبَةٍ مِّن قَبْلِ أَن يَتَمَآسَّا ذَٰلِكُمْ تُوعَظُونَ بِهِۦ وَٱللَّهُ بِمَا تَعْمَلُونَ خَبِيرٌ ۝ فَمَن لَّمْ يَجِدْ فَصِيَامُ شَهْرَيْنِ مُتَتَابِعَيْنِ مِن قَبْلِ أَن يَتَمَآسَّا فَمَن لَّمْ يَسْتَطِعْ فَإِطْعَامُ سِتِّينَ مِسْكِينًا ذَٰلِكَ لِتُؤْمِنُوا بِٱللَّهِ وَرَسُولِهِۦ وَتِلْكَ حُدُودُ ٱللَّهِ وَلِلْكَٰفِرِينَ عَذَابٌ أَلِيمٌ

"And those who pronounce *al-dhihaar* on their wives and then [wish to] go back on what they said— then [there must be] the freeing of a slave before they touch one another. That is what you are admonished thereby; and Allah is acquainted with what you do. And he who does not find [a slave] must fast for two months consecutively before they touch one another; and he who is unable must then feed sixty poor persons. That is for you to believe completely in Allah and His messenger; and those are the limits set by Allah. And for the disbelievers is a painful punishment" (*al-Mujaadilah* 3-4).

(3) The Expiation for Breaking One's Oath

Allah says,

لَا يُؤَاخِـذُكُمُ ٱللَّـهُ بِـاللَّغُوِ فِـيٓ أَيۡمَـٰنِكُـمۡ وَلَـٰكِـن يُؤَاخِـذُكُم

بِمَـا عَقَّـدتُّمُ ٱلۡأَيۡمَـٰنَ فَكَفَّـٰرَتُـهُۥٓ إِطۡعَـامُ عَشَـرَةِ مَسَـٰكِينَ مِـنۡ

أَوۡسَـطِ مَـا تُطۡعِمُونَ أَهۡلِيكُـمۡ أَوۡ كِسۡوَتُهُمۡ أَوۡ تَحۡرِيرُ رَقَبَةٖۖ فَمَن لَّمۡ

يَجِـدۡ فَصِيَـامُ ثَلَٰثَـةِ أَيَّـامٖۚ ذَٰلِـكَ كَفَّـٰرَةُ أَيۡمَـٰنِكُـمۡ إِذَا حَـلَفۡتُمۡۚ

وَٱحۡفَظُوٓاْ أَيۡمَـٰنَكُمۡۚ كَذَٰلِكَ يُبَيِّنُ ٱللَّهُ لَكُمۡ ءَايَـٰتِهِۦ لَعَلَّكُمۡ تَشۡـكُرُونَ

"Allah will not impose blame upon you for what is meaningless in your oaths, but He will impose blame upon you for [breaking] what you intended of oaths. So its expiation is the feeding of ten needy people from the average of that which you feed your [own] families or clothing them or the freeing of a slave. But whoever cannot find [or afford it] must then fast three days. That is the expiation for oaths when you have sworn them. But guard your oaths. Thus does Allah make clear to you His signs that you may be grateful" (*al-Maaidah* 89).

(4) The Expiation for Breaking a Vow

It is the same as the expiation for breaking an oath.

Al-Bukhari records that the Prophet (peace be upon him) stated,

مَنْ نَذَرَ أَنْ يُطِيعَ اللَّهَ فَلْيُطِعْهُ وَمَنْ نَذَرَ أَنْ يَعْصِيَهُ فَلَا يَعْصِهِ

"Whoever has made a vow in obedience to Allah should obey Allah. Whoever has made a vow for something in disobedience to Allah should not disobey Him." (Recorded by al-Bukhari.) The Prophet (peace be upon him) also said,

لَا نَذْرَ فِي مَعْصِيَةٍ وَكَفَّارَتُهُ كَفَّارَةُ يَمِينٍ

118

"There is not to be [any fulfillment of a vow] that is an act of disobedience. And its expiation is the expiation of breaking an oath."[1]

(5) The Expiation for One who Has Intercourse with His Wife While She is Having Her Menses

Ibn Abbaas narrated that the Prophet (peace be upon him) stated concerning a man who had intercourse with his wife while she was on her menses,

يَتَصَدَّقُ بِدِينَارٍ أَوْ بِنِصْفِ دِينَارٍ

"He should give in charity one *deenaar*[2] or half of a *deenaar*." (Recorded by Abu Dawood, al-Tirmidhi, al-Nasaai, ibn Maajah and Ahmad.[3])

(6) What the Fasts of Arafah and Ashooraa Expiate

Abu Qataadah said: The Messenger of Allah (peace be upon him) was asked about fasting the Day of Arafah [the 9ᵗʰ of Dhul-Hijjah]. He said,

يُكَفِّرُ السَّنَةَ الْمَاضِيَةَ وَالْبَاقِيَةَ

"It expiates [the minor sins] of the previous year and the coming year." (Recorded by Muslim.)

Abu Qataadah also narrated that the Messenger of Allah (peace be upon him) was asked about fasting the Day of Ashooraa [the 10ᵗʰ of Muharram] and he stated,

---

1 Recorded by Ahmad, al-Nasaai, Abu Dawood, al-Tirmidhi and ibn Maajah. According to al-Albani, this hadith is *sahih*. See al-Albani, *Sahih al-Jaami*, vol. 2, p. 1253.—JZ

2 The *deenaar* was the form of gold currency during the time of the Prophet (peace be upon him).

3 All of these collectors have similar hadith but not necessarily with that exact wording or meaning. According to al-Albani, this hadith is *sahih*. See al-Albani, *Sahih Sunan Abi Dawood*, vol. 1, p. 51.—JZ

يُكَفِّرُ السَّنَةَ الْمَاضِيَةَ

"It expiates [the minor sins] of the previous year." (Recorded by Muslim.)

It is the sunnah to fast in addition to the tenth of Muharram the ninth of Muharram as has been recorded by Muslim.

(7) What the Prayers Expiate

Abu Huraira narrated that the Prophet (peace be upon him) said,

الصَّلاةُ الْخَمْسُ وَالْجُمْعَةُ إِلَى الْجُمْعَةِ كَفَّارَةٌ لِمَا بَيْنَهُنَّ مَا لَمْ تُغْشَ

الْكَبَائِرُ

"The five daily prayers and the Friday Prayer until the Friday Prayer are an expiation for what is between them as long as a person does not perform the major sins." (Recorded by Muslim.)

(7) What the Pilgrimage and *Umrah*[1] Expiate

Abu Huraira narrated that the Prophet (peace be upon him) said,

الْعُمْرَةُ إِلَى الْعُمْرَةِ كَفَّارَةٌ لِمَا بَيْنَهُمَا وَالْحَجُّ الْمَبْرُورُ لَيْسَ لَهُ جَزَاءٌ إِلاَّ

الْجَنَّةُ

"One *umrah* until the next *umrah* is an expiation for what is between them. The Hajj performed properly and accepted by Allah will have no other reward than paradise." (Recorded by al-Bukhari and Muslim.)

---

[1] The *umrah* is the lesser pilgrimage that may be performed throughout the year.—JZ

He also narrated that the Messenger of Allah (peace be upon him) said,

مَنْ حَجَّ فَلَمْ يَرْفُثْ وَلَمْ يَفْسُقْ رَجَعَ كَمَا وَلَدَتْهُ أُمُّهُ

"Whoever performs the pilgrimage and commits no lewd speech or evil returns [being free of sin] like the day on which his mother gave birth to him." (Recorded by al-Bukhari and Muslim.)

(9) The Expiation for Useless Speech in a Gathering

Abu Huraira reported that the Messenger of Allah (peace be upon him) stated,

مَنْ جَلَسَ فِي مَجْلِسٍ فَكَثُرَ فِيهِ لَغَطُهُ فَقَالَ قَبْلَ أَنْ يَقُومَ مِنْ مَجْلِسِهِ

ذَلِكَ > سُبْحَانَكَ اللَّهُمَّ وَبِحَمْدِكَ أَشْهَدُ أَنْ لا إِلَهَ إِلاَّ أَنْتَ أَسْتَغْفِرُكَ

وَأَتُوبُ إِلَيْكَ > إِلاَّ غُفِرَ لَهُ مَا كَانَ فِي مَجْلِسه

"Whoever sits in a gathering that contains much useless speech and then says before he gets up from that setting, 'Exalted are You, o Allah, and to You is the praise. I bear witness that there is none worthy of worship but You. I seek Your forgiveness and repent to You,' forgiven for him will be what took place in that gathering." (Recorded by al-Tirmidhi.[1])

(26) The Virtues of Seeking Forgiveness

(1) Allah says,

---

[1] According to al-Albani, this hadith is *sahih*. See al-Albani, *Sahih al-Jaami*, vol. 2, p. 1065. The words have been transliterated already as *dhikr* #85.—JZ

وَٱسْتَغْفِرْ لِذَنْبِكَ وَسَبِّحْ بِحَمْدِ رَبِّكَ بِالْعَشِيِّ وَٱلْإِبْكَـٰرِ

"Ask forgiveness for your sin and exalt [Allah] with praise of
your Lord in the evening and in the morning" (*Ghaafir 55*).
   (2) The Messenger (peace be upon him) also said,

مَنْ لَزِمَ الِاسْتِغْفَارَ جَعَلَ اللّهُ لَهُ مِنْ كُلِّ ضِيقٍ مَخْرَجًا وَمِنْ كُلِّ هَمٍّ

فَرَجًا وَرَزَقَهُ مِنْ حَيْثُ لَا يَحْتَسِبُ

"Whoever sticks to [or continues in] seeking forgiveness,
Allah makes for him a way out of every difficulty, a relief
from every distress and provisions from where he did not
expect them." (Recorded by Abu Dawood.[1])
   (3) Therefore, a Muslim must seek Allah's forgiveness
often in the manner that is well known since this has a great
effect in erasing sins. And the Prophet (peace be upon him)
used to seek forgiveness often to the point that he would seek
Allah's forgiveness one hundred times in a day. This was the
case although all of his previous and later sins were forgiven
for him. One of the ways of asking forgiveness is to state the
words of the "leader of the ways of seeking forgiveness" as
was previously given. Another way is to say,

أَسْتَغْفِرُ اللّهَ الْعَظِيمَ الَّذِي لَا إِلَهَ إِلاَّ هُوَ الْحَيَّ الْقَيُّومَ وَأَتُوبُ إِلَيْهِ

"I seek forgiveness from Allah, the Great, the One besides
whom there is none other worthy of worship, the Ever-Living,
the All-Sustaining. And I repent to Him." (Recorded by al-
Tirmidhi.[2]) Or one may also say,

رَبِّ اغْفِرْ لِي وَتُبْ عَلَيَّ إِنَّكَ أَنْتَ التَّوَّابُ الرَّحِيمُ

---

[1] According to al-Albani, this hadith is weak. See al-Albani, *Dhaeef al-Jaami*, p.
841.—JZ
[2] This is from a hadith about what one should say when going to bed. However,
according to al-Albani and al-Hilaali, this hadith is weak. See al-Albani, *Dhaeef al-
Jaami*, p. 825; al-Hilaali, vol. 1, p. 266.—JZ

"Lord, forgive me and relent towards me, verily, You are the Most Relenting, the Merciful.[1]" (Recorded by al-Tirmidhi.[2])

(27) The Virtues of Supplications

(1) Allah says,

وَقَالَ رَبُّكُمُ ٱدْعُونِيٓ أَسْتَجِبْ لَكُمْ

"And your Lord says, 'Call on me and I shall respond to you'" (*Ghaafir* 60).

(2) The Messenger of Allah (peace be upon him) said,

الدُّعَاءُ هُوَ الْعِبَادَةُ

"Supplication is the [essence of] worship." (Recorded by Abu Dawood.[3])

(3) The Prophet (peace be upon him) also said,

مَنْ سَرَّهُ أَنْ يَسْتَجِيبَ اللَّهُ لَهُ عِنْدَ الشَّدَائِدِ وَالْكَرْبِ فَلْيُكْثِرِ الدُّعَاءَ فِي الرَّخَاءِ

"Whoever is pleased to have Allah respond to him during times of hardship and tribulations should increase his supplications during times of ease." (Recorded by al-Tirmidhi.[4])

(4) The Prophet (peace be upon him) preferred comprehensive supplications and he would leave other types. (Recorded by Abu Dawood.[5])

---

[1] *Dhikr* #126: *rabbi-gfir lee wa tub 'alayya ɛinnaka ɛanta-tawwaabu-raheem.*

[2] According to al-Hilaali, this hadith is *sahih*. See al-Hilaali, vol. 2, p. 973.—JZ

[3] According to al-Albani, this hadith is *sahih*. See al-Albani, *Sahih al-Jaami*, vol. 1, p. 641.—JZ

[4] According to al-Albani, this hadith is *hasan*. See al-Albani, *Sahih al-Jaami*, vol. 2, p. 1078.—JZ

[5] According to al-Hilaali, this hadith is *sahih*. See al-Hilaali, vol. 2, p. 934.—JZ

(5) One of the supplications that the Prophet (peace be upon him) would say often was,

رَبَّنَا آتِنَا فِي الدُّنْيَا حَسَنَةً وَفِي الآخِرَةِ حَسَنَةً وَقِنَا عَذَابَ النَّارِ

"O our Lord, grant us good in this life and good in the Hereafter. And save us from the punishment of the Fire.[1]" (Recorded by al-Bukhari.)

(6) The Mother of the Faithful, Umm Salamah (may Allah be pleased with her) was asked what supplication the Messenger of Allah (peace be upon him) would make the most when he was with her and she said,

يَا مُقَلِّبَ الْقُلُوبِ ثَبِّتْ قَلْبِي عَلَى دِينكَ

"O [You] who turns the hearts, confirm my heart upon Your religion." (Recorded by al-Tirmidhi.[2])

The Etiquette of Supplications

(1) One should begin one's supplications by praising Allah and saying prayers upon the Prophet (peace be upon him). One should end one's supplications in the same manner, followed by saying, *Ameen.*

(2) One should seek a means of approach to Allah by extolling His most beautiful names and exalted attributes, by mentioning one's righteous deeds or by asking pious people to supplicate on one's behalf.

(3) One should seek those times, places and noble situations for supplication. These include: the Night of Power and Decree, the last third of the night, at the end of the obligatory prayers, at the time of rain, in the midst of the battle ranks while fighting for the sake of Allah, the last hour on Friday, while prostrating, the day of Arafah, the month of Ramadhaan, while between the black stone and the door of

---

[1] *Dhikr #127: rabbanaa aatinaa fee-dunyaa hasanatan wa fee-l-aakhirati hasanatan wa qinaa 'adhaaban-naar.*

[2] According to al-Hilaali, this hadith is *sahih* due to its supporting evidence. See al-Hilaali, vol. 2, p. 945.—JZ

the Kaabah, while at Muzdalifah, while going between al-Safa and al-Marwa and so forth.

(4) It is recommended to face the *qiblah* (direction of the prayers), raise one's hands and say the supplication three times.

(5) Lower one's voice and avoid exaggeration in one's speech.

(6) Have one's heart present and aware, be sincere in one's submission and pleas and do not be hasty with respect to the response.

(7) One should be deliberate in the request and certain of the response. One should not think the question too great and, furthermore, one should have good expectations of Allah. One should not say, for example, "O Allah, forgive me if You wish."

(8) One should only eat from what is permissible, correct the wrong done to others and repent to Allah.

(9) One should not supplicate against oneself, one's children, one's wealth or one's servant. The Messenger of Allah (peace be upon him) stated,

لَا تَدْعُوا عَلَى أَنْفُسِكُمْ وَلَا تَدْعُوا عَلَى أَوْلَادِكُمْ وَلَا تَدْعُوا عَلَى
أَمْوَالِكُمْ لَا تُوَافِقُوا مِنَ اللَّهِ سَاعَةً يُسْأَلُ فِيهَا عَطَاءٌ فَيَسْتَجِيبُ لَكُمْ

"Do not supplicate against yourselves. Do not supplicate against your children. Do not supplicate against your wealth. It may be that your supplication coincides with a time in which Allah grants what is being asked and He responds to you." (Recorded by Muslim.) In the version by Abu Dawood, the following additional words are found, "Do not supplicate against your servants."

(10) One should not invoke Allah's face except for when one is asking for Paradise.

Those Whose Supplications are Answered

a) One in dire need.

b) One who is being wronged, even if he is a disbeliever.

c) A parent against or for his child.

d) A just ruler.

e) A pious son.

f) A Muslim who supplicates for his brother in his absence.

g) A fasting person until he breaks his fast.

h) A traveler until he returns

Note

Due to the importance of words of remembrance and their effect on a Muslim in his life, we suggest to the reader to get more information about this topic by consulting al-Nawawi's *al-Adhkaar* and its commentary, *Al-Futoohaat al-Rabaaniyyah* by ibn Alaan.

And may the prayers and blessings of Allah be upon Muhammad, his family and his Companions.

Translator's References

Akhdar, Hayaat. *Mauqif al-Islaam min al-Sihr.* Jeddah: Dar al-Mujtama. 1995.

Al-Albani, Muhammad Naasir al-Deen. *Dhaeef al-Jaami al-Sageer.* Beirut: al-Maktab al-Islaami. 1988.

-----*Dhaeef Sunan al-Tirmidhi.* Beirut: al-Maktab al-Islami. 1991.

-----*Ghaayat al-Maraam fi Takhreej Ahaadeeth al-Halaal wa al-Haraam.* Beirut: al-Maktab al-Islami. 1985.

-----*Sahih al-Adab al-Mufrad li-l-Imaam al-Bukhaari.* al-Zarqaa, Jordan: Dar al-Sideeq. 1994.

-----*Sahih al-Jaami al-Sagheer.* Beirut: al-Maktab al-Islami. 1986.

-----*Sahih Sunan Abi Dawood.* Riyadh: Maktab al-Tarbiyyah al-Arabi li-Duwal al-Khaleej. 1989.

-----*Sahih Sunan ibn Maajah.* Riyadh: Maktab al-Tarbiyyah al-Arabi li-Duwal al-Khaleej. 1986.

-----*Sahih Sunan al-Nasaai.* Riyadh: Maktab al-Tarbiyyah al-Arabi li-Duwal al-Khaleej. 1988.

-----*Sahih Sunan al-Tirmidhi.* Riyadh: Maktab al-Tarbiyyah al-Arabi li-Duwal al-Khaleej. 1988.

-----*Sahih al-Targheeb wa al-Tarheeb.* Riyadh: Maktabah al-Maarif. 1988.

-----*Silsilat al-Ahadeeth al-Saheeha.* Damascus: al-Maktab al-Islaami. 1979. Vol. 1.

Al-Arnaoot, Abdul Qaadir. Footnotes to al-Mubaarak ibn al-Atheer. *Jaami al-Usool fi Ahaadeeth al-Rasool.* Maktabah al-Halwaani. 1970.

Al-Arnaoot, Shuaib. Footnotes to al-Faarisi, Ali. *al-Ihsaan fi Taqreeb Saheeh ibn Hibbaan.* Beirut: Muasassah al-Risaalah. 1987.

----- Footnotes to Abdul Rahmaan ibn Rajab. *Jaami al-Uloom wa al-Hikm.* Beirut: Muasassah al-Risaalah. 1991.

al-Ashqar, Umar. *Aalim al-Sihr wa al-Shaoowadhah.* Kuwait: Maktabah al-Falaah. 1989.

Baali, Waheed. *al-Saarim al-Bataar fi al-Tasaddee lil-Saharati-l-Ashraar.* Jeddah: Maktaba al-Sahaaba. 1992.

Al-Daaraqutni, Ali ibn Umar. *al-Ilal al-Waaridah fi al-Ahaadeeth al-Nabawiyyah.* Riyadh: Dar Taibah. n.d.

al-Damaini, Misfur. *Al-Sihr: Haqeeqatuhu wa Hikmuhu...* 1991.

al-Faarisi, Ali. *al-Ihsaan fi Taqreeb Saheeh ibn Hibbaan.* Beirut: Muasassah al-Risaalah. 1987.

al-Hilaali, Saleem. *Sahih Kitaab al-Adhkaar wa Dhaeefuhu.* Madinah: Maktabah al-Ghurabaa al-Athariyyah. 1997.

Ibn Baaz, Abdul Azeez. *Majmoo Fatawa wa Maqaalaat Mutanwaah.* Riyadh: Maktabah al-Maarif. 1992.

ibn Hajr, Ahmad. *Fath al-Bari bi-Sharh Sahih al-Bukhari.* Beirut: Dar al-Fikr. 1993.

Ibn Muhammad, Fauzi ibn Abdullah. *Al-Fulk fi Fadhl Soorah al-Mulk.*

ibn al-Qayyim, Abu Bakr. *Jalaa al-Afhaam fi Fadhl al-Salaat wa al-Salaam ala Muhammad Khair al-Anaam.* Dammam, Saudi Arabia: Dar ibn al-Jauzi. 1997.

ibn al-Sunee, Ahmad. *Kitaab 'Amal al-Yaum wa al-Lailah.* Beirut: Muasassah al-Kutub al-Thaqaafiyyah. 1988.

Al-Jaleemi, Sayyid ibn Abbaas. Footnotes to Muhammad ibn Isa al-Tirmidhi. *al-Shamaail al-Muhammadiyyah wa al-Khasaail al-Mustafiyyah.* Beirut: Muasassah al-Kutub al-Thaqafiyyah. 1992.

Maroof, Bashaar and Shuaib al-Arnaoot. *Tahreer Taqreeb al-Tahdheeb.* Beirut: Muasassah al-Risaalah. 1997.

Al-Nasaai, Ahmad ibn Shuaib. *al-Sunan al-Kubra.* Beirut: Daar al-Kutub al-Imiyyah. 1991.

al-Nawawi, Yahya. *al-Adhkaar.* Riyadh: Riaasah Idaarat al-Bahooth al-Ilmiyyah wa al-Iftaa wa al-Dawah wa al-Irshaad. 1981.

al-Salafi, Saalim. Footnotes to Ahmad ibn al-Sunee. *Kitaab 'Amal al-Yaum wa al-Lailah.* Beirut: Muasassah al-Kutub al-Thaqaafiyyah. 1988.

Salmaan, Mashhoor Hasan. Footnotes to Abu Bakr ibn al-Qayyim. *Jalaa al-Afhaam fi Fadhl al-Salaat wa al-Salaam ala Muhammad Khair al-Anaam.* Dammam, Saudi Arabia: Dar ibn al-Jauzi. 1997.

Smart, J. *Teach Yourself Arabic: A Complete Course for Beginners.* Chicago: NTC Publishing Group. 1992.

al-Tabaraani, Sulaimaan. *Kitaab al-Duaa.* Beirut: Daar al-Bashaair al-Islaamiyah. 1987.

-----*al-Mujam al-Kabeer.* Cairo: Maktaba ibn Taimiya. n.d.

Zarabozo, Jamaal. *Commentary on the Forty Hadith of al-Nawawi.* Boulder, CO: Basheer Company for Publications and Translations. Forthcoming Allah willing.

Index of Quranic Verses Cited

al-Faatiha – p. 66
al-Baqara – p. 21
   152 – p. 4
   155-157 – pp. 73-74
   255 – pp. 8-9, 23, 41,
      69, 89
   264 – p. 97
   283 – p. 95
   285-286 – pp. 15-16
ali-Imraan – p. 21
   110 – p. 112
   190-200 – p. 16
al-Nisaa 1 – p. 110
   110 – p. 47
   148 – p. 91
al-Maaidah 89 – p. 118
   44 – p. 106
al-Anaam 108 – p. 102
al-Araaf 54 – p. 89
   117-119 – pp. 69-70
Yoonus 79-82 – p. 70
Hood 102 – p. 94
   114 – p. 6
al-Rad 28 – p. 4
al-Nahl 116 – p. 99
al-Israa 32 – p. 105
   36 – p. 98
al-Kahf – pp. 21-22
   1-10 – p. 22
   39 – p. 62

Taha 65-69 – pp. 70-71
al-Hajj 30 – p. 95
al-Noor 19 – p. 107
   23 – p. 107
Luqmaan 6 – pp. 111-112
   18 – pp. 95-6
al-Ahzaab 56 – p. 19
al-Saaffaat 143-144 – pp. 4-5
al-Zumar 60 – p. 99
Ghaafir 55 – p. 122
   60 – p. 123
al-Hujuraat 11 – pp. 96-97
   12 – p. 92
Qaaf 37 – p. 1
   39 – p. 6
   45 – p. 1
al-Dhaariyaat 55 – p. 1
al-Najm 32 – p. 104
al-Mujaadilah 3-4 – p. 117
al-Mulk – p. 16, 22
al-Qiyaamah – p. 22
al-Mursalaat – p. 22
al-Dhuhaa 10-11 – p. 97
al-Teen – p. 22
al-Kaafiroon – p. 44, 69
al-Ikhlaas – p. 10, 23, 41, 44, 69
al-Falaq – p. 10, 23, 41, 69, 89
al-Naas – p. 10, 23, 41, 69, 89

General Index

Ablution, words and etiquette 30-31

Abusive language 100-103

Adhaan – see call to prayer

Afflicted, being 59

Angry, when getting 59

Arafah, fast of 119

Ashoorah, fast of 119

Backbiting 92

Bathroom etiquette 28-30

Bequests = Wills

Bewitched 69-72

Boasting 95-96

Bribery 109-110

Call to prayer, words related to 34-36

Charitable Endowmens 114-115

Clothing and Dressing 31-32

Clouds 53

Concealing faults 107-108

Cursing = Abusive Language

Death and dying, words related to 72-73, 76-80

Debt 51-52, 61

Dhihaar, expiation for 116-117

Difficult matter 50-51

Difficulties = Hardship

Displeasing occurrence 51

Distress, words for 49-50, 63-66

Dog barking 58

Donkey braying 58

Doubts about faith 52

Drinking = Eating and drinking

Eating and drinking 85-87

Evil Eye 67-69

False testimony 95

Fasting, words related to 42-43

Forgiveness, virtues of seeking 121-122

Fortune-tellers 105-06

Funeral and graves 76-80

Gathering, upon finishing 58, 121

Graves = Funerals and graves

Hardship and difficulties, words related to 48-49, 52, 63-66, 73-76

House, leaving and entering, words for 32-33

Ill = Sick

Imitation of others 110-111

Innovations and heresies 108-109

Kin, keeping ties 110

Late Afternoon

　definition 6-7

　words said 7-15

Laughing 56-57, 94

Love, when one loves another 56

Lying 98-00

Magic = Bewitched

Marketplace 60

Marriage 88-89

Mocking a Muslim 96-97

Moon

　moonrise 55

　seeing new moon, 55

Morning

　definition 6-7

　words said 7-15

Mosque

　heading to mosque at

Fajr time 47
words related to 36-38
Music = Singing and music
Nighttime
words said 15-16
Oaths, expiation for breaking 117-118
Omens 109
Ordering good and eradicating evil
112-113
Prayers, words said afterwards 38-42
Prophet (peace be upon him)
when to pray for him
19-21
Prostration
of reading Quran 46
of thankfulness 46
Quran, reciting 21-23
prostration 46
Rain 54-55
Remembrance of Allah
benefits of 5-6
virtues of 4-5
Repentance, prayer of 47
Rooster crowing 58
Salat = see prayers
Salat al-Istikhaarah 44-45
Satan, feeling his effect 53
Seeing
something amazing 61-62
something disliked 63
something one loves 62
Sick, the 66-67
Singing and music 111-112
Sleep, words and acts for, 23-27
Sneezing 57
Speech

guarding one's 89-100
speaking too much 90-91
Supplications
etiquette of 124125
whose are answered 125-126
virtues of 123-24
Swearing by other than Allah 97-98
Tale-carrying 92-93
Terms, disapproved of 104
Thunder 54
Traveling, words related to 81-85
Vows 106-107
Expiation for breaking
118-119
Wills 113-114
Winds 54
Worry = see distress
Yawning = 58
Youngster, words to protect 53

ORDER FORM

To order any of the books published by Al-Basheer Company, simply copy or tear out this page, fill in the order form below and send it with a check or money order for the appropriate amount to: Al-Basheer Company, 1750 30th St. PMB #440, Boulder, CO 80301

Qty	Title	Price	Amount
	Marital Discord – Saalih Sadlaan	$6.00	
	He Came to Teach You Your Religion – Jamaal Zarabozo	$11.00	
	The World of the Jinn and Devils – Umar al-Ashqar	$11.00	
	Words of Remembrance and Words of Reminder w/ tape – Saalih al-Sadlaan	$9.00	
	The Fiqh of Marriage in the Light of the Quran and Sunnah - Saalih al-Sadlaan	10.00	
	How to Approach and Understand the Quran - Jamaal Zarabozo	16.00	
	Commentary on the Forty Hadith of al-Nawawi (3 volumes) - Jamaal Zarabozo (Special Shipping Charge = $8.00)	80.00	
	Subtotal		
	CO Residents add 7.41% Sales Tax		
	Postage for inside U.S.: $3.75 for first book, $1.00 for each additional book; for orders of over $100 pay only 10% as shipping charge		
	TOTAL		

Name _____

Address _____

City _____ ST _____ ZIP _____

Phone number _____

ORDER FORM

To order any of the books published by Al-Basheer Company, simply copy or tear out this page, fill in the order form below and send it with a check or money order for the appropriate amount to: Al-Basheer Company, 1750 30th St. PMB #440, Boulder, CO 80301

Qty	Title	Price	Amount
	Marital Discord – Saalih Sadlaan	$6.00	
	He Came to Teach You Your Religion – Jamaal Zarabozo	$11.00	
	The World of the Jinn and Devils – Umar al-Ashqar	$11.00	
	Words of Remembrance and Words of Reminder w/ tape – Saalih al-Sadlaan	$9.00	
	The Fiqh of Marriage in the Light of the Quran and Sunnah - Saalih al-Sadlaan	10.00	
	How to Approach and Understand the Quran - Jamaal Zarabozo	16.00	
	Commentary on the Forty Hadith of al-Nawawi (3 volumes) - Jamaal Zarabozo (Special Shipping Charge = $8.00)	80.00	
		Subtotal	
	CO Residents add 7.41% Sales Tax		
	Postage for inside U.S.: $3.75 for first book, $1.00 for each additional book; for orders of over $100 pay only 10% as shipping charge		
		TOTAL	

Name _____

Address _____

City _____ ST _____ ZIP _____

Phone number _____